The
Beastly Book of
Dinosaur Action Toys

The
Beastly Book of
Dinosaur Action Toys

Alan & Gill Bridgewater

TAB BOOKS Inc.
Blue Ridge Summit, PA

FIRST EDITION
FIRST PRINTING

© 1992 by **TAB Books**.
TAB Books is a division of McGraw-Hill, Inc.

Library of Congress Cataloging-in-Publication Data

Bridgewater, Alan.
    The beastly book of dinosaur action toys / by Alan and Gill
Bridgewater.
      p.   cm.
    Includes index.
    ISBN 0-8306-2161-X (pbk.)
    1. Wooden toy making 2. Toys, Mechanical. 3. Dinosaurs in art.
I. Bridgewater, Gill. II. Title.
TT174.5.W6B727 1992
745.592—dc20   92-5294
                                                   CIP

TAB Books offers software for sale. For information and a catalog, please contact TAB Software Department, Blue Ridge Summit, PA 17294-0850.

Acquisitions Editor: Stacy Varavvas Pomeroy
Book Editor: Susan D. Wahlman
Director of Production: Katherine G. Brown
Book Design: Jaclyn J. Boone
Cover Design and Illustration: Graphics Plus, Hanover, PA   HT5

Contents

Acknowledgments

We would like to thank Stacy Varavvas Pomeroy for thinking up the idea of dinosaur toys—it's beautifully beastly! We also would like to thank our two sons, Glyn and Julian, for their enthusiasm. Finally, we would like to thank Tracy A. Emmison for the Humbrol paints and Henry Taylor Tools for the gouges and lathe tools.

Introduction

WELCOME TO THE WHIRLING, twirling, wibble-wobble world of *The Beastly Book of Dinosaur Action Toys*! Welcome to a weird and wonderful world inhabited by a whole diorama of clicking, clacking, trundling, brooming, driving, cycling, dashing, daredevil dinosaur toys. Welcome to a timeless toymaking world of chassis boards, wheels, axles, cams, bearing blocks, brushes, screws, washers, rivets, glue, and paint. Mmm . . . can't you just smell the wood, the paint, and the polish?

Why dinosaur toys? The answer is beautifully beastly—children love dinosaurs. Or, perhaps we should say, both kids and adults seem to be fascinated by the whole subject of dinosaurs. This interest is evident in the growing numbers of dinosaur characters that walk across our television screens and jump out from the pages of our books. Comics feature dinosaur heroes; cartoons have dinosaurs; and a wonderful series, *Dinosaurs*, made it to hit status on primetime TV. Of course, we can't forget the Flintstones—good old Fred and Wilma—and all their dinosaur pets. City museums are full of dinosaur bones; toy-store shelves sag under the weight of dinosaur toys; we could go on and on. The plain and simple fact is, dinosaurmania is sweeping the globe.

Children love to hear all the scary, hair-tingling facts and figures: Dinosaurs ruled the world for more than 160 million years; the last dinosaur died out 60 million years before the first humans evolved; the longest dinosaur was about 90 feet from nose to tail; and the biggest dinosaur checked in at about 70 tons. Also, most children enjoy the tortuous tongue-twisting dinosaur names: protosuchus, ankylosaurus, proceratops, camptosaurus, hadrosaurus, and all the rest—aren't they beautiful! If it's big, monstrous, and covered with a multitude of lumps, bumps, horns, spikes, and scales, most kids are going to think it's great fun.

The Beastly Book of Dinosaur Action Toys translates the current interest in the revered reptiles into fun and exciting action toys. Each of the 16 projects opens with a little yarn about the particular dinosaur, and then goes straight into all the finger-tingling wooden toymaking procedures. You'll find project pictures, gridded and scaled working drawings with cross-sections and details, tool and material lists, gridded and scaled design templates, wonderful step-by-step drawings, and painting grids. The how-to text is carefully considered, with a special hints section at the end of every project. A tools, tips, and techniques glossary appears at the end of the book. All in all, we've included enough skill-stretching woodworking techniques, ideas, designs, and details to keep even the most adventurous toymaker busy and satisfied. No matter what your particular interest—working on the scroll saw, drilling, whittling, woodturning between centers, woodturning with a four-jaw chuck, painting, or designing—each and every project has been painstakingly put together so that the toys can be shaped, modified, and adjusted to suit your own skill level and tool capability.

The tales at the beginning of each project breathe life into the dinosaur toys and give them names, personalities, thoughts, and ambitions—and they're great fun! These tongue-in-cheek sketches are as much for the toymaker as for the child. They will give you something to chuckle about while you're making the toys. Once you have enjoyed the wonderfully creative craft of toymaking, you can derive that extra measure of pleasure when, on handing over the toy, you tell the lucky recipient your own personalized, edited-to-suit-the-child version of the dinosaur's story.

What child will be able to resist a tale about Tracy the Tireless Triceratops, or Cedric the Cycling Saltopus, or Amy the Amiable Ankylosaurus, or any one of the other dinosaur toy characters. If you like dinosaurs, if you like toys, if you like exploring a full range of woodworking techniques, if you like children, and if you like the notion of sitting a kid on your knee and spinning a good-fun, told-in-a-moment dinosaur yarn, then you are going to enjoy this book.

1

Bones the
Confused Dinosaur

POOR OLD BONES is really mixed up and misunderstood! First he was named brontosaurus—meaning "thunder lizard"—then he got jumbled in with a sauropod called camarasaurus, and then he was renamed apatosaurus—meaning "deceptive lizard."

All the confusion started when he was found by the famous Yale collector Othniel C. March, out in the American Wild West, way back in 1877. When scientists put him together, they were so excited, they gave poor old Bones the wrong head. But that wasn't the worst of it. Not content with losing bits and pieces, they couldn't come to any agreement as to who and what Bones was. They agreed that he was heavier than a diplodocus, and that he wasn't as tall as brachiosaurus. Could it be, they wondered, that since he had a lot in common with the camarasaurus, he was indeed a member of the same family? Bones was so traumatized by the whole affair that he lost his head completely.

The good news is, in 1979 two experts found the original head, and decided that Bones was not at all like a camarasaurus, but more like his old friend the diplodocus. The bad news is, that although Bones is one of the best known of all the dinosaurs, the text books still can't decide whether to call him brontosaurus or apatosaurus, or even camarasaurus. Is it any wonder that Bones is confused?

Tools and materials

- A sheet of best-quality, white-faced, 1/4-inch-thick multicore plywood, about 12×18 inches, for all the cutouts—allowing for cutting waste
- A length of 1/4-inch-diameter dowel
- A small amount of Super Glue fast-drying adhesive
- A pair of plastic eyes used for soft toys like rag dolls and teddy bears
- Acrylic paint in green, yellow, red, and black
- A small quantity of clear, high-shine varnish
- A pencil and ruler
- A sheet of workout paper

- A sheet of tracing paper
- An electric scroll saw with a pack of spare blades
- A pillar, bench, or press drill with $\frac{1}{8}$-inch- and $\frac{1}{4}$-inch-diameter bits
- A small pin hammer, sometimes called a light cross-peen hammer
- A quantity of $\frac{1}{2}$-inch-long panel pins, brads, or nails
- A pair of long-nosed grips or pliers
- A small amount of two-tube wood filler
- A quantity of Plasticine modeling material and a number of scrap wood spikes or pencils, to use as painting supports
- A pack of graded sandpapers
- A roll of double-sided masking tape
- A couple of long-haired brushes, one broad and one fine-point

Looking and planning

Bones is an articulated toy in the classic Crandall tradition. That is, like the jointed toys that were made in America in the nineteenth century by a family called Crandall, this toy is constructed of thin-section plywood, with the various pieces pivoted so that they can be moved around and set in position. As to why toys of this character are so popular, we think it is because the play activity is so uncomplicated and naive. Kids enjoy bending the limbs and setting them in funny poses. One moment Bones looks like he's running, then sitting up (FIG. 1-1), then standing on his head, and so on. By setting the stay-put jointed neck, tail, and legs in different positions, kids can create an infinite number of humorous poses.

Look at the working drawings (FIGS. 1-2 and 1-3), and consider how, as far as technique is concerned, Bones is a straightforward, easy-to-make toy. A little bit of scroll saw work, drilling a dozen or so holes, and a little bit of painting and putting together—what could be simpler? That said, we think it's only fair to point out that the actual putting-together stage is finger-twisting. The work is not so much complicated as it is tricky because a lot of small pieces need to be carefully related one to another.

You put the linked joints together like a chain, in a one-two-one-two sequence: first a single piece, linked to a pair of pieces, linked to a single piece, and so on. What makes the toy stay put once it is set in a position is the tight friction-fit of the pivot dowels in the holes.

Note how, depending on where they occur, the pivot dowels variously stick out about $\frac{1}{4}$ inch from the surface, are flush with the surface, or are cut and wedged.

Setting out the design and first cuts

After you have studied the design templates (FIG. 1-4), draw the designs to full size and make a good, clear tracing. Hinge the traced pattern pencil-side-down to the face of the sheet of multicore plywood and use a sharp 2H pencil to carefully pencil-press transfer (see glossary) the traced lines through to the wood. Make sure that the transferred lines and the pivot hole centerpoints are clear and well established. Spend time getting it just right.

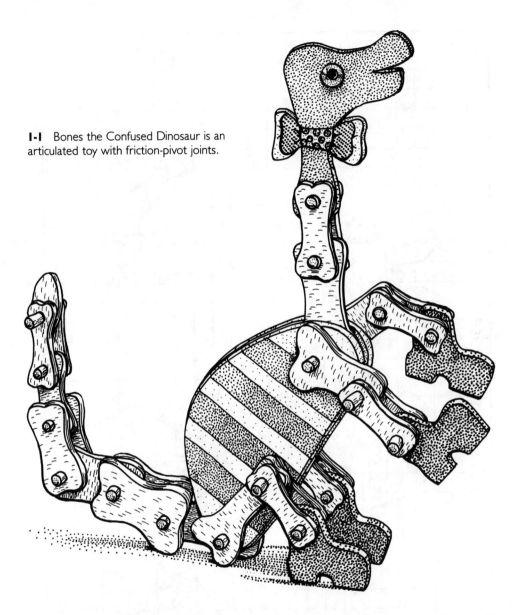

1-1 Bones the Confused Dinosaur is an articulated toy with friction-pivot joints.

When you are happy with the transferred images, take the wood to the scroll saw and swiftly cut it down into easy-to-handle pieces. At this stage, don't try to get close to the drawn lines; just cut about 1/4 inch to the waste side of the lines.

Grouping, pinning, and fretting out

Take the rough-cut pieces and set them out on your work surface. You should have 36 components in all—a single head, 4 matched boots, 2 matched bodies, 4 matched front leg calves, 4 matched back leg calves, 4 pairs of double links, 5 single links, 2 matched front leg thighs, 2 matched back leg thighs, and 4 washers.

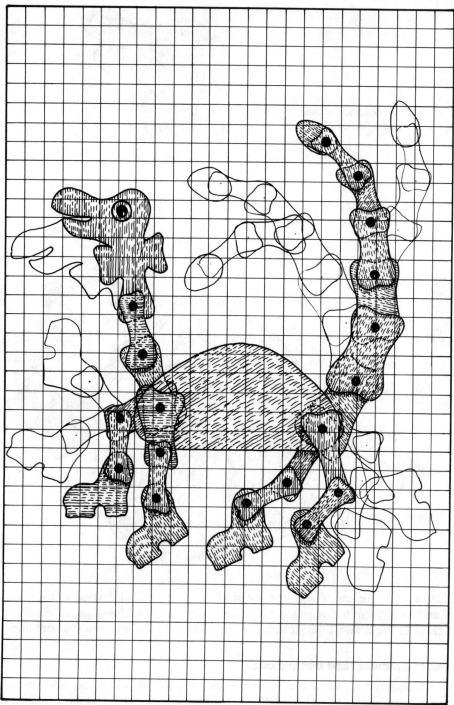

1-2 This working drawing shows the toy's range of movement. The scale is two grid squares to 1 inch.

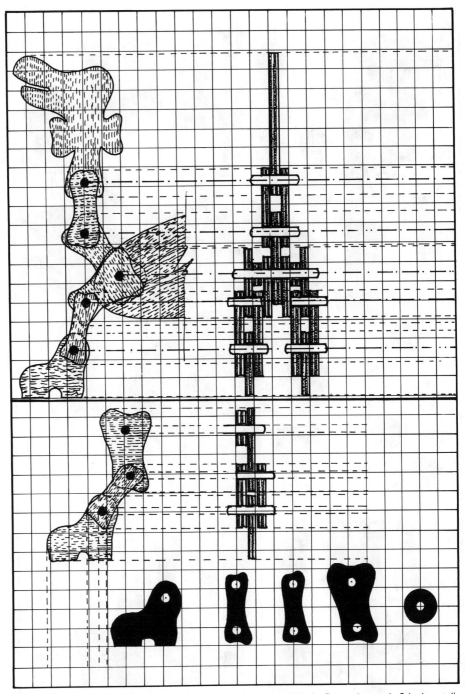

I-3 Working drawing. At a scale of two grid squares to 1 inch, Bones is nearly 9 inches tall. Side view detail and cross section (top); side view detail of a foot and cross section (middle); design templates (bottom).

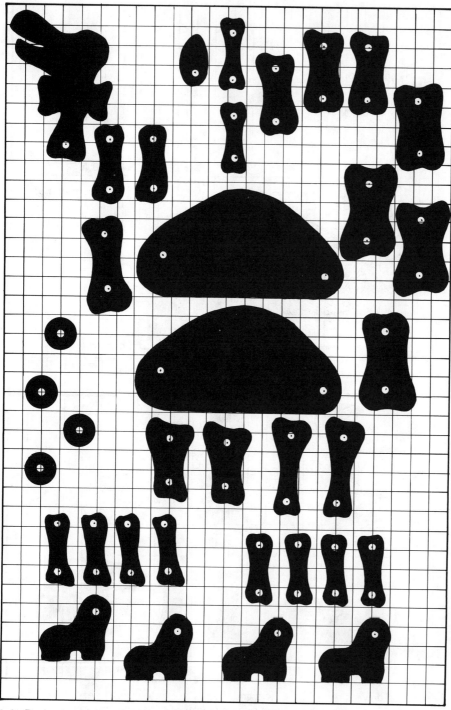

I-4 Design templates at a scale of two grid squares to 1 inch.

Arrange and group the pieces in singles or in stacks so that a clear image is uppermost. Then take the hammer and the panel pins, and pin the layers together (FIG. 1-5). Bear in mind that you need to remove the 1/2-inch pins at a later stage. With a two-layer stack, all you do is bang the pin through the top layer and half-way through the bottom layer so that about 1/8 inch of the pin stands proud. Make sure the pins are set within the drawn profile, but away from the pivot-hole areas, and the bottom face of each of the stacks is smooth and free from pin points.

With all the stacks well organized and pinned together, take them to the scroll saw. Check that the blade has the teeth pointing downwards, towards the cutting surface; adjust the tension; and check that the machine is in good order.

One stack at a time, hold the pieces flat on the cutting surface, and gently guide them into the moving blade. Allowing for slight distortion of the blade, feed the wood in a counterclockwise direction so that the line of cut travels clockwise around the profile (FIG. 1-6). Using a scroll saw is relatively simple, as long as you

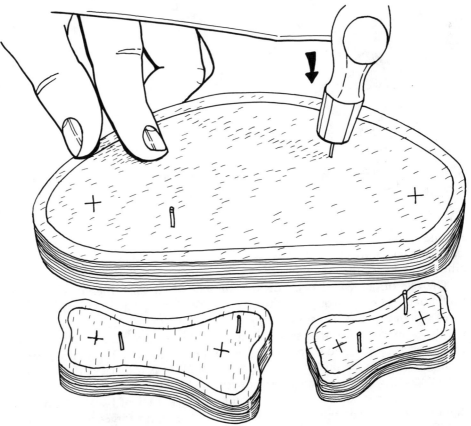

1-5 Arrange and group the pieces in stacks, and use pins to make a temporary fix. Make sure the traced profile is uppermost.

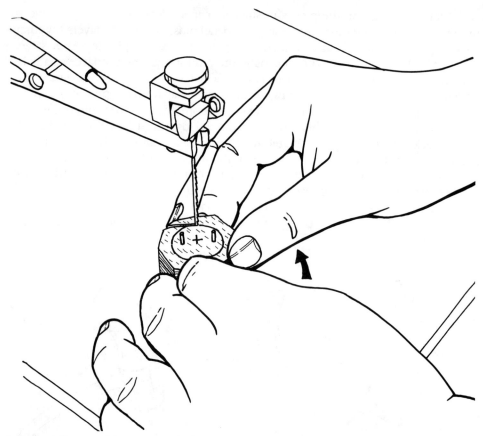

1-6 Feed the wood in a counterclockwise direction so that the line of cut travels clockwise around the profile.

keep the wood moving at a steady pace so that the blade is presented with the next line of cut, and as long as you make sure that the line of cut is always slightly to the waste side of the drawn line.

The rate of cut will depend on the number of layers in the stack and the amount of pressure that you put on the wood. Try to apply a gentle pressure. This way of working results in a slow rate of cut, but then the resulting cut face is so smooth, clean, and crisp that sanding time is reduced to a minimum. Continue cutting out one stack, and then another, until the job is done. If the blade keeps breaking, then you are pushing too hard or the blade is too slack. If the wood starts to scorch, you are pushing too slow or the blade needs to be changed. Be warned—if you are beginner, you are going to break a lot of blades! Don't get caught short—be ready with plenty of spares. *Note:* Don't forget to slacken the blade tension when you have finished and switched off the saw.

Drilling

When you have cut out all the pieces, clear away the clutter and move to the pillar or press drill. With the cutouts still pinned together in stacks, start to bore out the 1/4-inch-diameter pivot holes. One piece or stack at a time, support the cut wood on a level scrap of wood, make sure that the position of the pivot holes is clearly marked, and run the hole through the wood (FIG. 1-7, top right).

After you have drilled all the holes, use long-nosed grips, or pliers, to gently ease out all the temporary fixing pins. Break the stacked layers down into individual cutouts. Patch the pin holes and any damage with wood filler (FIG. 1-7, bottom).

Finally, drill out the single 1/8-inch-diameter eye hole and give the cutouts a swift rubdown with fine sandpaper. Cut back excess filler, sharp edges, and whiskers of loose grain.

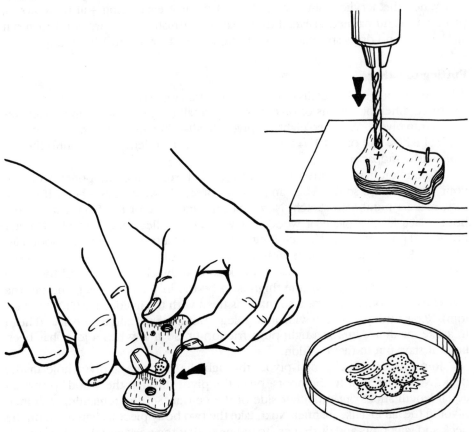

1-7 Support the work on a scrap of wood while at the same time making sure that the drill is set at right angles to the working face (top right). Carefully fill the nail holes and any damaged areas (bottom).

Painting and varnishing

Once you have all of the cutouts drilled and rubbed down, wipe away the dust and move to the clean, dry, warm area you have set aside for painting and varnishing. Cover your work surface with newspaper, and set each of the cutouts on a little Plasticine-and-stick stand to prepare for painting. Squash down a small ball of Plasticine to make the stand base, place a stick or splinter of waste into the Plasticine, and spike the cutout to be painted onto the end of the stick. (See **painting** in the glossary.) You need one stand for each small cutout and two for the main body part.

Before you start, study the painting grid (FIG. 1-8). Paint the boots bright red, the head green, the bow tie yellow, and the body stripes green and yellow. Lay on two coats, with a light sanding between coats. When the yellow bow tie is dry, take a fine-point brush and paint in the red polka dots—small dots on the inner bow and large dots on the center knot—then paint in all the black line details.

When the acrylic paint is completely dry, give everything—all the cutouts, plain wood and painted—several thin coats of varnish. Make sure you brush out all the runs and drips and that the pivot holes are clear of varnish buildup.

Putting together

Take a fresh look at the details of the working drawings (FIGS. 1-2 and 1-3) and note the three different lengths of pivots. With a small saw, cut the 1/4-inch-diameter dowel into pivots. You need eighteen pivots in all—fifteen at 1 1/4 inches long, two at 2 1/2 inches, and one at 1 3/4 inches. Cut the pivots to length and round the cut ends with sandpaper.

When you have the pivots cut and rounded, set all the components out on your work surface so that you can plan out precisely what goes where. If necessary, make a numbered sketch. Now, starting with one of the front legs, take a boot, place it on a piece of wood that you have drilled with 3/8-inch-diameter holes, and push or tap a 1 1/4-inch-long dowel pivot halfway through the boot (FIG. 1-9, top). Repeat the procedure with the lower end of the front thigh bone. Next, take the two matched calf bones and link-and-sandwich the boot and the thigh bone. Decide which face of the thigh is to be the inside of the leg, and tap the dowel back through the wood so that it is flush with the inside face (FIG. 1-9, bottom). Repeat this procedure with all four legs. Build the tail and the neck and head in a like manner. Aim for a tight-push friction-fit, so that when a joint has been bent, it stays put in that position.

Run one of the 2 1/2-inch pivots through the body-neck pivot hole in the neck. Now, just as with the boots, push the pivot through the wood so that an equal length sticks out on either side of the cutout. Set the remaining 2 1/2-inch pivot in the tail in a like manner. Next, take the two body pieces, align them on the neck and tail pivots and push them together so that the neck and the tail are sandwiched and contained. Finally, slide the wooden washers and the legs in place on the ends of the through-body pivots.

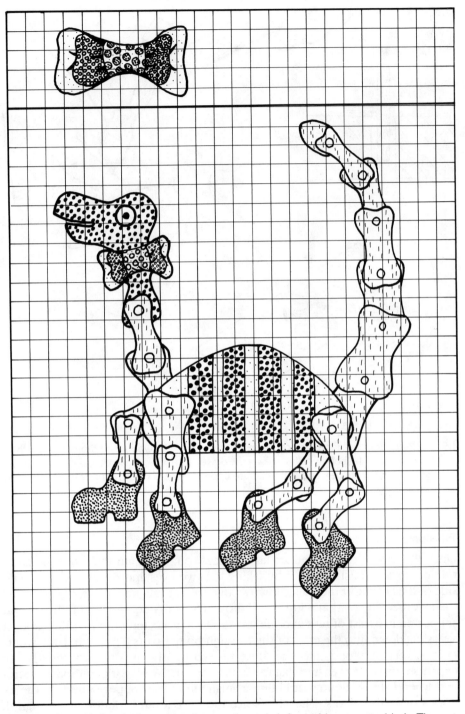

1-8 Painting grid. For the bow tie at the top, the scale is four grid squares to 1 inch. The rest of the illustration is drawn at a scale of two grid squares to 1 inch (bottom).

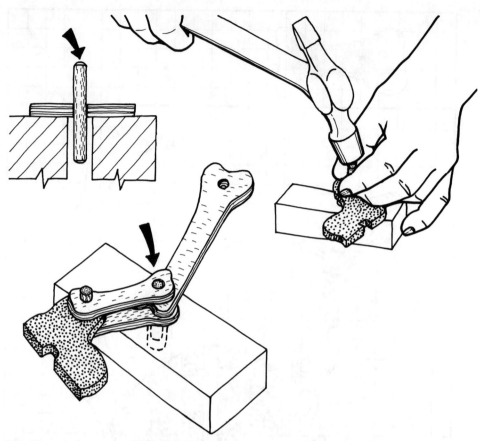

1-9 Place the boot over the ³/8-inch-diameter predrilled scrap wood, and tap the 1¹/4-inch-long dowel in place until the boot is halfway along the dowel (top). Decide which face of the thigh bone is to be the inside of the leg, and with that face uppermost, tap the dowel through until it is flush (bottom).

Finishing

Once the legs, neck, and tail are all in place, you can begin the satisfying task of tidying up and finishing. Start by taking the two eyes and fitting them on either side of the head. Cut the stalks down so that they are slightly shorter than ¹/8 inch, then fix them in position with a small drop of Super Glue. Next, with the dinosaur supported in a nest of rags and the top surfaces protected with masking tape, cut saw slots down into the ends of the through-body pivots (FIG. 1-10). Glue and tap little slivers of wood into the slots to expand the pivot ends slightly. The expanded pivot ends ensure that the limbs stay put. Now work methodically from end to end along the toy, dribbling a small amount of Super Glue into the exit points of all the pivots. The pivots need to have a tight friction-fit through the middle sandwiched cutouts and a fixed glue-fit on the outside layer.

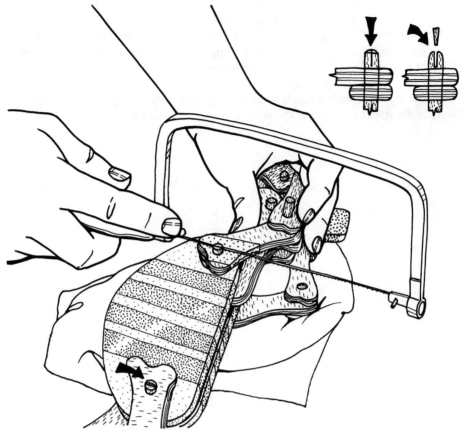

1-10 Protect the top of the leg with masking tape, and, with the workpiece cradled in a nest of rags, cut the saw slots down into the ends of the through-body pivots, and glue and tap little slivers of wood into the slots.

Finally, rub down any sharp edges and touch up any scuff marks, as well as the dowel ends, with varnish. When the work is completely dry, check on the movement, and give the whole toy a swift rubbing with a small amount of wax polish. Bones is now ready for his first stiff-jointed walk across the treacherous terrain of the playroom.

Hints

- When you are hammering the dowel through the layers of wood, support the cutouts on a piece of predrilled scrap, so that the dowel ends can run through without doing damage.
- All the pivot joints must have a good, tight friction-fit. To this end, make sure that your dowel diameter matches the size of your drill. When you are drilling out the holes, settle for a single in-and-out pass of the bit.

- If you like the idea of the toy, but want to change the scale to make it larger, also scale up the ply thickness and the dowel diameter.
- When you are choosing your scroll saw blades, go for a medium tooth size. If you have any doubts, have a tryout on some scrap wood. If you are using the correct size of blade, set at the proper tension, the resulting cutouts should be clean-cut and smooth-edged.
- To make working with a scroll saw easier, polish the cutting table with wax to reduce the friction between the sliding wood and the metal.

2

Noddy the Nodosaurus

THIS NODOSAURUS—pronounced node-oh-saw-rus, but known to her buddies as Noddy—likes to be pushed around. Now don't get us wrong—Noddy's not soft-headed. In fact, she's one of the toughest and roughest of all the dinosaurs. She's just a pushover when it comes to children. Looking at her heavy armor and knowing that she comes from a long line of aggressively defensive node-lizard dinosaurs, you certainly might think that Noddy is all set to rip your arms off. But underneath the skin, Noddy is kind, friendly, and altogether wonderful—especially with children. Don't worry about kids freeloading rides at Noddy's expense—her back is broad, she is strong, and she loves it. In fact, Noddy is the kind of dinosaur who likes nothing better than to be set down on the carpet and trundled around the house by a whole herd of kids. It's her idea of fun!

It has been a long, hard day. Noddy has been trundled up and down the garden path, scrambled across the lawn, zoomed along the hall, scooted around the bedroom, and then finally stunt-trundled at high speed into the toy cupboard—crunch! She's all ready to nod off, her nodule nodes are numb, her eyes are heavy, her casters are red hot, and she. . . yawn. . . .

Tools and materials
- A piece of easy-to-carve, straight-grained, knot-free, prepared wood, 24 inches long, 8 inches wide, and 4 inches thick (something like lime white pine or jelutong is ideal)
- Three heavy-duty casters or glides, like the kind used on large armchairs, made of noncorroding materials
- Brass screws to fit the casters
- A piece of heavy strap or belt leather, 8×4 inches
- A 40-inch length of ¹/₂-inch-diameter dowel
- A sheet of workout paper
- A sheet of tracing paper
- A large, flat-bladed, general-purpose saw

- A roll of double-sided tape
- A band saw
- A drawknife
- A rasp
- A twist brace with two Forstner drill bits—one $1^1/2$ to 2 inches in diameter, to fit the size of the casters, and one $1/2$ inch in diameter, for the dowel nodes
- A craft knife
- A quantity of two-tube resin glue, or something similar, to stick leather to wood
- A strong workbench and vise
- A pack of graded sandpapers
- A roll of 1-inch-wide masking tape
- A bradawl
- Acrylic paints in red and black
- A can of clear, high-shine varnish
- One broad and one fine-point brush

Looking and planning

Noddy the nodosaurus (FIG. 2-1) is a good-fun push-and-trundle toy. She is strong, she can put up with any amount of rough treatment, she makes a good-sized stand-in for a dog, her tail movement is intriguing, her back nodules are just right for young, grasping, learning hands, and, best of all, she is designed to be pushed, pulled, scooted, and trundled around the house. Noddy is the perfect toy for kids who like a lot of action.

From a woodworker's or toymaker's point of view, this project is particularly exciting because it involves the use of tools and skills for wood carving and creating free sculptural forms. That is to say, you rough out the block of easy-to-carve wood on the band saw, then shape and sculpt the blank with the drawknife and

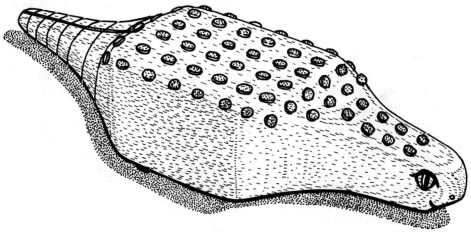

2-1 Noddy the Nodosaurus is a toddler's sit-on-and-scramble trundle toy.

rasp, and finally inset the surface with knobs, or nodes. If your woodworking pleasures tend towards carving, whittling, and sculpting, rather than, say, scroll saw work, then this project is for you.

Have a good long look at the working drawings (FIGS. 2-2 and 2-3), and see how, at a scale of one grid square to 1 inch, Noddy measures 22 inches long from nose to tail, 8 inches wide, and 4 inches high. Note the way the block is shaped so that the completed toy has a low, ground-hugging center of gravity. The top of the block is cut away, rounded, and reduced, so that the resulting broad-based form sits flat and low, with most of the weight below the centerline.

The three wheels, casters, or glides, can be a bit tricky to fit. You will place them at 120-degree intervals around a circle, set in drilled recesses, so that they are mostly hidden from view and the flat base is no more than about $3/4$ inch off the ground.

The tail is an interesting feature—just the sort of quirky fun that kids enjoy. You will cut, work, and laminate it in such a way that it can be flexed very slightly from side to side. Have a look at the details of the working drawings, and see the way the tail end is sawn along the centerline and cut into 1-inch slices, with the resulting half slices mounted symmetrically on either side of an inset leather-strap spine. Study the details and cross sections, and note the way the beautifully bumpy texture is created by setting a series of $1/2$-inch-long, $1/2$-inch-diameter, round-end dowel plugs into holes that are $1/4$ inch deep. Finally, draw the designs up to size and take tracings of the profile views.

Setting out the design

When you have studied the working drawings and made tracings of the profiles, set the 24-inch length of easy-to-carve, prepared wood out on the bench and check it over to make sure that it is free from warps, splits, and knots. For this project, the wood needs to be top-quality. If the wood contains loose, dead knots or splits that run into the end grain, or is faulted in any way, then look for another piece. *Note:* By prepared wood, we mean wood that has been planed on all faces.

With a pencil, label one of the 8-inch-wide faces TOP, and then label all the other faces: SIDE, HEAD, and TAIL. Draw crossed diagonals to fix the centerpoint of each face. Using the centerpoints as guides, draw centerlines that run from head to tail and from side to side around the block of wood.

Take the tracings of the various profiles, and carefully pencil-press transfer the traced lines through to the wood. When you have clearly set out the various views, shade in the areas of waste so that you'll have no doubt about what needs to be kept and what needs to be discarded (FIG. 2-4, top).

Drilling the caster holes

Once you have set out the design, flip the block of wood over so that the underside is uppermost, and use a pencil, ruler, and compass to establish the position of the three casters. (FIG. 2-3, middle). With the wood well-supported in the vise, take the brace and the 2-inch Forstner bit, and carefully sink the three flat-bottomed caster holes. Run the holes in to a depth of about 1 inch, and make sure that they

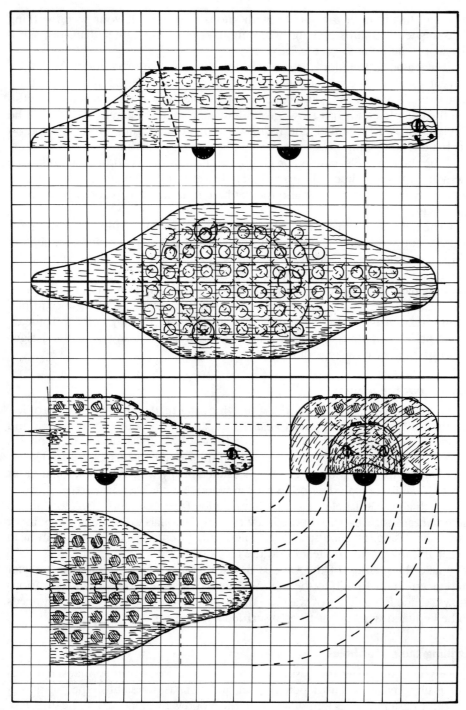

2-2 Working drawing. At a scale of one grid square to 1 inch, Noddy measures about 22 inches long, about 5 inches high from the ground to the top of the nodules, and 8 inches wide.

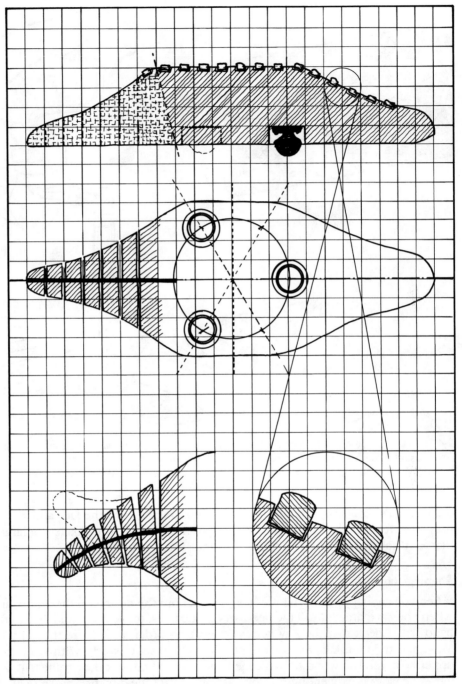

2-3 Working drawing. The scale is one grid square to 1 inch. The cross section shows the leather tail and casters (top). The underside view shows how the casters are set out on the circumference line of a 7-inch-diameter circle (middle). In the detail of the tail and nodules (bottom), the nodule inset (right) is at a scale of four squares to 1 inch.

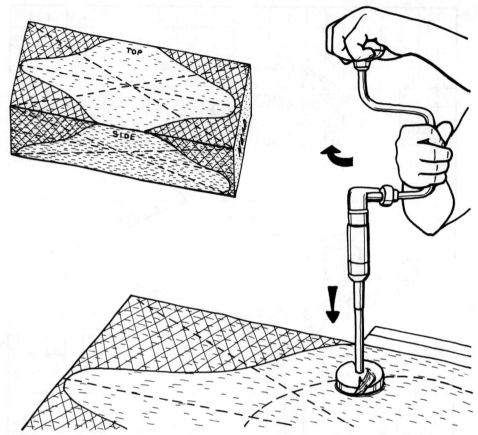

2-4 Pencil-press transfer the design profiles through to the wood and shade in the areas of waste (top). Use the 2-inch-diameter Forstner bit to run blind holes in to a depth of about 1 inch (bottom right). Make sure that the sinkings are level and at right angles to the working face.

are worked so that they run into the wood at right angles to the face and so that they are level (FIG. 2-4, right). *Note:* You might need to bore out smaller- or larger-diameter holes, depending on the design and size of your casters.

Shaping the body

When you are happy with the way you have set out the design on the wood, and when you have drawn in all the necessary guide lines, move the workpiece to the band saw. Check that the saw is in safe working order, make sure that all your loose hair and clothing are under control, and then set to work. With a side face uppermost, run the wood through the band saw and cut out the profile (FIG. 2-5, left). The work is easy enough, as long as you control the direction and rate of cut so that the sawn line is slightly to the waste side of the drawn line.

When you are done cutting the waste from the side, set strips of double-sided tape on the sawn faces and refit the lumps of waste to reconstruct the original

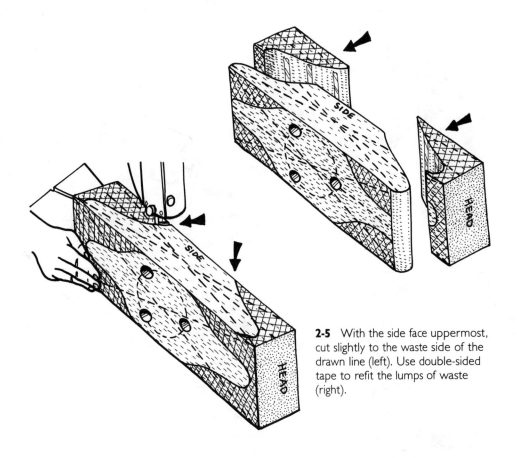

2-5 With the side face uppermost, cut slightly to the waste side of the drawn line (left). Use double-sided tape to refit the lumps of waste (right).

24-×-8-×-4-inch block (FIG. 2-5, right). Next set the wood on the band saw cutting table so that the top face is uppermost, and cut away all the waste you can see from the top view. Bear in mind that the top waste doesn't mark out the shape of the top of the body, but rather it sets out the shape of the largest profile—the bottom profile—as it is seen in top view.

Once you have achieved the basic flat-faced blank, remove the waste wood, clear the work surface of debris, and set to work with the drawknife, shaving away all the sharp angles. With the blank secured and angled in the vise so that the top face is uppermost, with the tail end pointing away from you (FIG. 2-6, bottom), run the drawknife from the top center to the nose, all the while cutting away the waste and working towards the envisioned form (FIG. 2-6, top). Repeat the process with the tail end. Don't be tempted to slash off great chunks, and don't be in too much of a hurry to finish. You'll do better if you slowly and carefully work a curve here and a curve there, stopping often to compare the workpiece with the working drawings, until gradually you see the body taking shape.

When you have what you consider to be a good, strong, nicely curved, flat-based shape, use the rasp to remove all the angles and facets left by the drawknife (FIG. 2-7, top). Finally, take the sandpapers and work through the grades—from

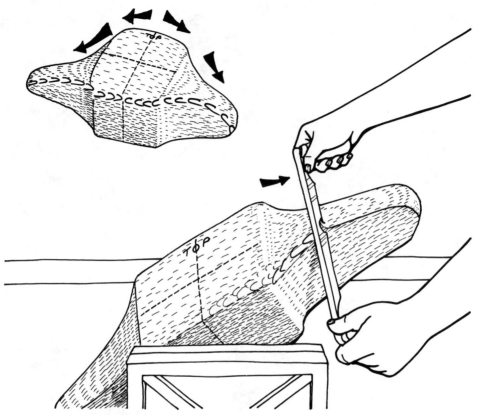

2-6 Secure the workpiece with its top face uppermost and the tail pointing away from you, and use the drawknife to shave away all the sharp angles (bottom). Work the drawknife from the center to the ends to remove the bulk of waste wood (top).

coarse through fine—until the surface is smooth and the grain begins to shine (FIG. 2-7, bottom).

Making the tail

Study the working drawings (FIG. 2-3) again until you have a clear understanding of how the tail end of the dinosaur should be worked and put together. Then flip the body shape so that the flat side is uppermost—the dinosaur will be on its back—and carefully establish all the guidelines that make up the design. Draw in the position of the spine and the six 1-inch slice lines around the tail. Take the workpiece back to the band saw. Support the body on a wedge-shaped piece of waste and angle it up at the nose so that the line of cut runs at an angle into the body. Then make a couple of side-by-side cuts along the line of the spine (FIG. 2-8, top). Aim to make a slot that is a tight-gripped fit for the leather strap.

Once you have a good, clean-cut spine slot, smear a generous amount of resin glue on both sides of the leather strap, slide it into the spine slot, and bind the tail with masking tape or twine. When the glue is dry, remove the binding and use a

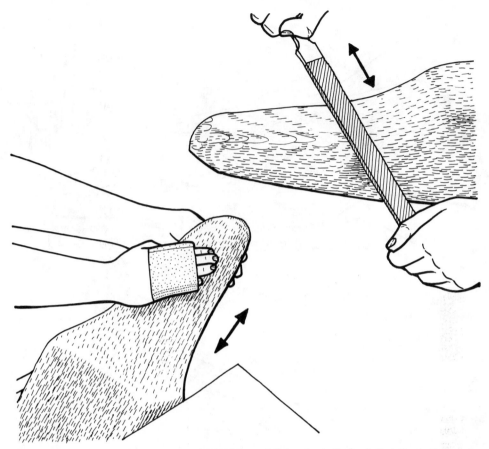

2-7 Use the rasp to remove any angles and facets left by the knife (top). Rub down the workpiece with the graded sandpapers until the surface is smooth and the grain begins to shine (bottom).

craft knife to trim the leather to shape. Then take the workpiece back to the band saw. With the workpiece held top-side-up, start at the tip of the tail and cut in the six slice lines at either side of the spine. Do one side of the tail at a time and be extra careful not to cut the leather (FIG. 2-8, bottom).

Fitting the nodules

Have another close look at the working drawings and details, and see how the nodules relate to a 1-inch-square grid. With one node at the center of each 1-×-1-inch square, the pattern of nodules runs over the back to the neck and tail.

Use a pencil and ruler to set out a few registration points. Then take the roll of 1-inch-wide masking tape and set the workpiece out with a 1-inch-square checkerboard grid. First run the tape from head to tail at 1-inch intervals—1-inch width of tape, 1-inch space, 1-inch width of tape, and so on—and then repeat the procedure across the width of the back. You should finish up with a crisscross grid pat-

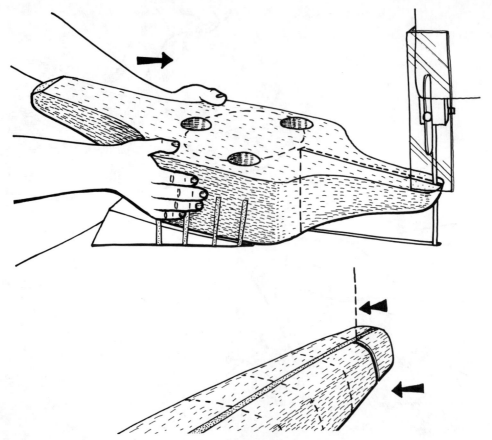

2-8 Support the workpiece on a wedge-shaped piece of waste so that it is presented to the saw blade at the desired angle. Make two side-by-side cuts along the tail length of the spine (top). Starting at the tip of the tail and working one side at a time, cut the slices that make the design of the tail (bottom). Be careful not to cut into the leather.

tern of tape with 1-inch squares of space between the crisscross grid marks. Decide where within the grid you want the nodules to be set, then draw crossed diagonals to fix the centerpoints of the selected squares (FIG. 2-9, left). Spike the centerpoints with a bradawl and remove the tape.

With the workpiece held securely on the bench, bore out the pattern of nodule holes with the brace and 1/2-inch Forstner bit (FIG. 2-9, right). When you have achieved the pattern of 1/4-inch-deep, 1/2-inch-wide holes, saw the dowel into 1/2-inch lengths and glue a nodule into each hole. First dribble a small amount of glue into a hole, take a 1/2-inch length of dowel and score the bottom with a knife, and then tap the dowel into the hole. The dowel should have a tight fit, a small amount of glue should ooze up from the score marks, and the dowel should stand proud of the surface of the workpiece by 1/4 inch. Continue until the pattern of nodules is complete.

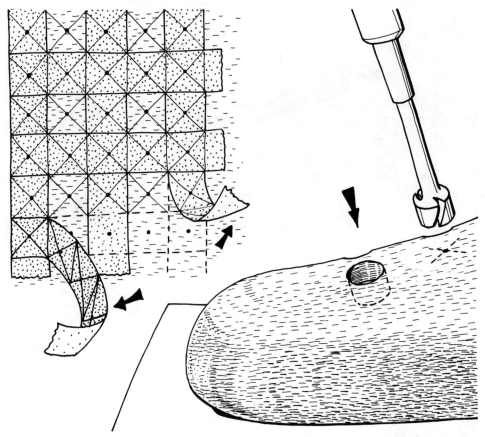

2-9 Run a masking tape grid across the curved surface, draw diagonals, and spike the center points with a bradawl (left). Use the bradawl centerpoint marks as a guide, and sink the pattern of nodule holes with a brace and a Forstner bit (right).

When the glue is dry, take the pack of graded sandpapers and a small block and rub the dowels down to a smooth, round-ended finish.

Painting and finishing

Wipe away all the dust and debris and remove the workpiece to the area set aside for painting. Study the painting grid (FIG. 2-10) and the project picture (FIG 2-1). Start by taking a fine-point brush and carefully painting each of the nodules bright red. Try not to dribble any paint over the body. If you need to apply more than one coat of paint to achieve good coverage, lightly sand the painted pieces between coats. Next, use both the black and red paint to paint in all the little details of the nose, mouth, and eyes—a red nose and mouth and black eyes. When the paint is dry, give the whole toy a swift rubdown with a fine-grade sandpaper to remove all the whiskers of grain, and then lay on a couple of coats of clear varnish. Don't forget to give the varnish a swift rubdown between coats. Finally,

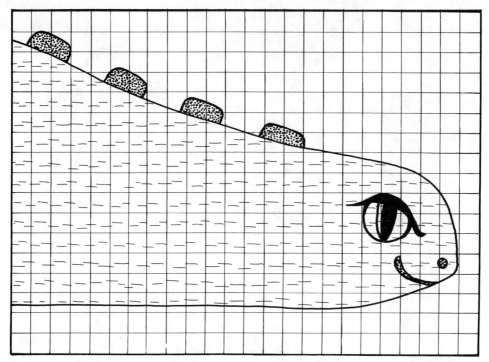

2-10 Painting grid. The scale is four grid squares to 1 inch. The nodules, nostrils, and mouth are painted red, the eyes black; then the whole toy is varnished.

screw the casters into the holes on the bottom, make good any scuff marks, and the job is done.

Hints

- If you can't obtain a piece of wood that is large enough, you can use smaller sections—say, four glued-together 2-×-2-inch pieces or two 4-×-4-inch sections—and then modify the design accordingly.
- For increased stability, but at the cost of some maneuverability, you could redesign the arrangement of the casters to have two wheels at the back and two wheels at the front.
- If you are worried about Noddy bumping into walls, furniture, pets, ankles, and the like, you could give her a complete wraparound plastic fender, or you could screw a couple rubber doorstop "horns" onto her nose.
- The tail is designed to flex ever so slightly so it doesn't trap little fingers. If you can't obtain the leather, you could settle for a strip of rubber or canvas, or even for pretend, scored joints and a rigid tail.

3

Dinosaur Puzzle

PUZZLING! Dinosaurs ruled the earth for more than 160 million years, and yet in all that time, they didn't come up with a satisfactory collective term for a group of dinosaurs. We all know about a pride of lions, a flock of sheep, a pack of dogs, a swarm of bees, and all the other collectives, but what about the poor old dinosaurs? It's a vexing question. Our dinosaurs have met here for no other reason than to iron out the problem of precisely what they should be called when they are so gathered.

And what a meeting! The stegosaurus kept treading on the protoceratops, the saltopus would not stop running up and down the stegosaurus's back, the deinonychus didn't know what day of the week it was, the psittacosaurus couldn't get along with the ankylosaurus, the scelidosaurus was feeling dyspeptic, the barosaurus could hardly squeeze his bulk in the door, and the triceratops was, er, confused.

Could it be that dinosaurs are so bad-tempered that they have never before met *en masse*? If that's the case—how about a disagreement of dinosaurs, or perhaps a dispersion of dinosaurs, or even a dishevelment. Ha! What about a disgruntlement of dinosaurs?

Tools and materials
- A sheet of best-quality, white-faced, 3/4-inch-thick, multicore plywood, 10×14 inches
- A pencil, ruler, compass, and set square
- An electric scroll saw (we use a Hegner)
- A small quantity of two-tube resin wood filler
- A small hand drill with a 1/8-inch-diameter bit
- A pack of graded sandpapers
- Acrylic paints (we used dark and light blue, yellow, green, and red)
- A small quantity of clear, high-shine varnish

- A medium-sized, soft-haired paintbrush
- A small amount of wax furniture polish

Looking and planning

This puzzle is a delightfully complete plaything. Each dinosaur is painted a bright color and they all fit into a clear varnish background frame (FIG. 3-1)—really beautiful! Children love that once the dinosaurs have been tipped out of their frame, they become separate playthings in their own right. The individual dinosaurs can be balanced one on top of another, or drawn around with colored pencils, or used as templates and pressed into dough to make cookies, or used as watercolor stamp prints, or played with in the sandbox, or cuddled in bed, or even arranged on a shelf. Perhaps the best fun of all, for toddlers, is deciding how to set the bold, brightly colored dinosaur profiles back into place to complete the puzzle. This toy offers any number of exciting play possibilities.

Have a look at the working drawings (FIG. 3-2) and details, and see how the drilled saw-blade holes have been placed and designed so that they become rather satisfying push-and-poke finger holes. Note how, with the working drawing at an approximate scale of about two-and-a-half grid squares to 1 inch, the puzzle measures 9 inches wide and $13^{1}/_{2}$ inches long. If you want to make the puzzle larger or smaller, all you do is adjust the scale to suit. As to skill level, because the design is so crisp and bold, the scroll saw work must be managed with extra care and precision. Be warned—if you make an untidy mess with one or other of the saw cuts, it will show. For the dinosaurs to be able to stand upright, the saw cut must run through the wood at right angles to the working face. Note how some of the dinosaurs have saw-slot mouths and hole-punched eyes.

Setting out the design and drilling

When you have studied the working drawing (FIG. 3-2), which you will also use as the design template, draw the design up to full size and take good, clear, crisp tracings. Use a soft pencil to do the tracing.

Make sure that the multicore plywood is free from splits, delaminations, stains, knots, and tears. Use the pencil, compass, ruler, and square to draw out on the wood the shape of the total outer frame—the curved-corner shape of the background board. Making sure that the tracing is perfectly aligned within the frame, hinge the tracing to the top edge of the plywood with a few tabs of masking tape. When you are happy with the arrangement, take a hard pencil and pencil-press transfer the traced lines through to the wood (FIG. 3-3, right). Finally, take the drill and the $^{1}/_{8}$-inch bit, and sink pilot saw-blade holes through each of the little half-circle finger holes (FIG. 3-3, left).

Using the scroll saw

With the design clearly established on the face of the plywood, you will take on the make-or-break task of cutting out the forms with the scroll saw. Bearing in mind that if you have to stop and start on a straight cut, the line is going to be

3-1 This puzzle features stand-up dinosaur cutouts.

3-2 Working drawing, design template, and painting grid. The scale is about two and a half grid squares to 1 inch. The names of the dinosaurs, left to right, top to bottom, are psittacosaurus (pale blue), ankylosaurus (red), stegosaurus (dark blue), saltopus (yellow), triceratops (pale blue), protoceratops (green), deinonychus (dark blue), barosaurus (yellow), allosaurus (red), and scelidosaurus (green).

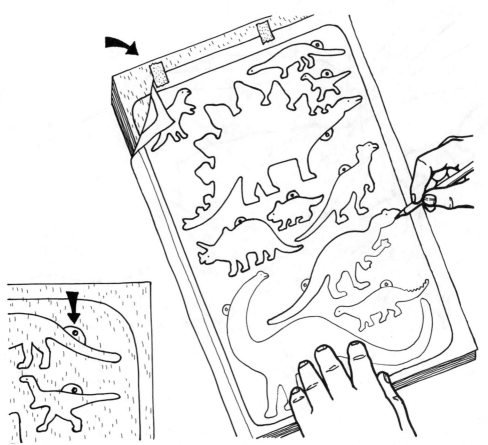

3-3 Hinge the tracing down with tabs of masking tape and pencil-press transfer the lines of the design through to the wood (right). Use the $1/8$-inch-diameter bit to run the pilot holes through each of the little half-circle finger holes (left).

jerky, stepped, or perhaps even downright curvy, warn friends and family that you are going to use the scroll saw and need to work undisturbed. Scroll saw work is easy enough as long your attention is one hundred percent on the job at hand. Also make sure that the saw is fit for use. To this end, give the cutting table a swift rubbing over with wax polish, fit and tension a new fine-toothed saw blade, check that the cutting table is set correctly at right angles to the blade, and generally see to it that the machine is in good working order.

Switch on the power and set to work cutting out the straight-edged, curved-corner frame. Just feed the workpiece into the moving blade, all the while making sure that the cut line is slightly to the waste side of the drawn line and that the moving blade is timely presented with the line of next cut. If you work at a gentle, easy pace, you will avoid tearing the wood, and the workpiece will leave the saw with the cut edges so perfectly smooth and shiny that they won't need much of a rubdown.

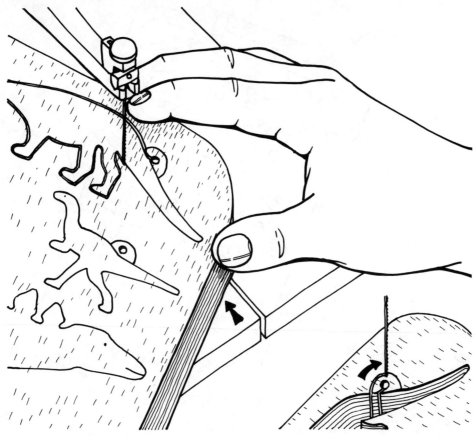

3-4 Pass the blade through the pilot holes, refit and retension the blade, and then cut out the dinosaur profiles (left). Finish by cutting away the finger hole (bottom right).

When you have cut out the total frame shape, unhitch the top end of the saw blade, pass the blade through one of the drilled pilot holes, and refit and retension the blade. Then switch on the power and very carefully cut out the first dinosaur profile (FIG. 3-4, left). Remove the cutout and finish by cutting away the little half-circle of the finger hole (FIG. 3-4, bottom right). Unhitch the blade, and work the next dinosaur shape in a like manner. Continue until you have completed all ten cutouts that make up the puzzle. Finally cut the mouths and punch the eyes as shown in FIG. 3-2.

Rubbing down, painting, and finishing

When you have worked all ten dinosaur cutouts, then comes the task of rubbing the work down to a good finish. First check the sawn edges for cavities, delaminations, and tears. If you find any problems, now is the time to make them good with the two-tube resin filler or the glue. Use as small an amount of filler as possible. Wait for the filler to dry, and then take the graded sandpapers and rub down all the sharp corners of the animals, the holes, and the frame edge to a smooth, slightly round-cornered finish. For tight, difficult-to-get-at areas, cover a stick with sandpaper (FIG. 3-5, top left) and use it as you would a small file (FIG. 3-5, bottom left).

When the workpiece is completely smooth-faced and round-cornered to the touch, brush away all the dust and debris and move to the dust-free area that you have set aside for painting. Have a look at the painting grid (FIG. 3-2), and note how we have painted the psittacosaurus pale blue, the ankylosaurus red, the saltopus yellow, the stegosaurus dark blue, the triceratops pale blue, the proceratops green, the deinonychus dark blue, the allosaurus red, the barosaurus yellow, and the scelidosaurus green (see the glossary for the **painting grid color code**). Arrange all the paints and brushes so that they are close at hand. You don't need to set up a drying frame or line, because by the time you have painted the animals with the acrylics, the paint will be more or less touch-dry. You will only need to stand the painted animals on a clean, smooth surface.

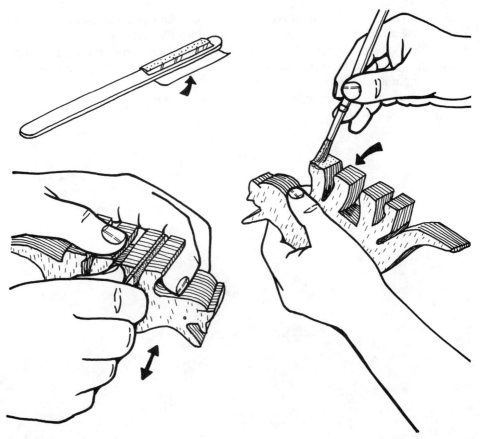

3-5 Cover a stick with sandpaper to make a sanding tool (top left). Use the sanding stick to rub down difficult-to-get-at areas (bottom left). Starting at the feet, paint the edges first (right).

Hold the cutouts between your thumb and index finger, and lay the paint on in smooth, thin coats. Starting at the feet (FIG. 3-5, right), paint the edges, then one face, then the other. By the time you have painted all ten animals, the first ones should be dry enough for you to lightly sand and repeat the process.

When the paint is dry, rub the dinosaurs down with the fine-grade sandpaper and give the whole toy—all faces and edges—a couple of coats of clear varnish. Be careful not to leave thick blobs or buildup in tight-curve cavities.

Finally, when the varnish is completely dry, give the edges of all the frame holes a wax polishing so that the dinosaurs are a smooth, easy fit.

Hints

- If you only have 1/4-inch-thick plywood, consider bonding three sheets together to make the total 3/4-inch thickness.
- Be careful when you are using the scroll saw. Don't go so slowly that you friction-burn the wood or go so fast that the blade tears the face of the wood as it exits. Have a tryout with a scrap of plywood before you begin cutting the good piece.
- If you do need to fill tears or edge cavities, you can use a wood-colored filler or a small amount of scroll saw dust mixed with PVA glue.
- Cut edges must be at right angles to the working face of the wood. Make sure that the scroll saw blade is well tensioned, and the cutting table is set so that it is at right angles to the line of the saw blade.
- Be careful when you are painting to avoid building up too much paint on the edges of the animals.

4

Dashing Dinosaur Driver

THIS STENONYCHOSAURUS, known by his racing buddies as Hot Rod Nike-O, is fast—very fast! The only thing slow about Nike-O is his cumbersome formal name. But then again, what's in a name? When he was found in 1932, in southern Alberta, Canada, by a certain Dr. C. M. Sternberg, the good doctor, looking for a single name to describe the dinosaur's many qualities and characteristics, came up with stenonychosaurus, pronounced sten-oh-nike-o-saw-rus, meaning narrow-clawed.

With his small, long, slender, lightly built body, long arms and legs, large eyes, and large brain, Nike-O is, of all the dinosaurs, the fastest, the most active, and the most intelligent.

Not for Nike-O the daily grind of slowing munching his way through tons of shoots, roots, and fruits. He is a swift-moving, meat-eating, cool dude who enjoys living life in the fast lane.

Nike-O settles back in his curved dash, high-performance, streamlined, sling-shot, 1902 hot-rod Oldsmobile special. He can feel the blood coursing through his veins as the 3-hp engine roars into action. They are under starter's orders, the flag is up, the crowd is silent. Varoooom—he's away!

Tools and materials

- A sheet of best-quality, white-faced, 3/8-inch-thick multicore plywood, 4×7 inches, for the chassis base, allowing for a small amount of waste
- Scraps of best-quality, white-faced multicore plywood, 1/4-inch and 3/4-inch thick, for the windshield and the bonnet or tonneau
- A 6-inch length of 2-×-2½-inch beech for the main body of the car
- A 20-inch length of easy-to-turn wood, 2¼ square inches, for the dinosaur figure and the four wheels (we used beech)
- A 9-inch length of 3/8-inch-diameter dowel, for the two axle rods
- Eight 3/4-inch-long brass dome-headed screws, for the various fixings
- A small amount of white PVA wood glue

- Acrylic paints in yellow, blue, green, red, white, and black
- A small can of clear, high-shine varnish
- A pencil, ruler, and square
- A sheet of tracing paper
- A sheet of workout paper
- A woodturning lathe
- A four-jaw chuck to fit the lathe
- A good selection of turning tools
- A compass, a pair of dividers, and a pair of calipers
- A small straight saw
- A scroll saw
- Three flat chisels—1 inch, $3/8$ inch, and $1/8$ inch
- A small knife for whittling
- A small spoon gouge or small U gouge
- A drill with $1^{1}/2$-, $3/8$-, $1/4$-, and $1/8$-inch-diameter bits
- A pack of graded sandpapers

Looking and planning

Toys of the stenonychosaurus-in-a-car type are a delight on many counts (FIG. 4-1). They are strong; they can be put together from small, inexpensive, easy-to-find scraps; the shapes are bold and uncomplicated; the construction techniques are basic; and, best of all, their movements are both funny and efficient. What child or adult could not find pleasure in a car that moves with a curious stop-and-start, wibble-wobble action?

Look at the working drawings (FIG. 4-2) and see how the movement is created by having the axles set off-center on the wheels. The design is beautifully straight-forward, in that the various parts all easily screw or slot together to make a nicely fitting whole. Note for example, how once the axles have been slid into the under-side body channels, they are held and contained by the chassis base plate, which is screwed directly to the underside of the body. The windshield slides into a channel cut on the topside of the car body. See also how the bonnet, or tonneau, is screw-fitted directly to the top of the car body. In fact, all the parts fit and slot into each other so easily and directly that with a little bit of modification, the car could be redesigned as a knock-down construction toy. Easy to make, nice to look at, and fun to play with—what else do we require of a good toy?

Making the car chassis

Have a good, long look at the working drawing (FIG. 4-2), step-by-step details, and the project picture (FIG. 4-1). When you have a clear understanding of how the toy needs to be worked and put together, set all your wood out on your work surface and check it over for possible problems. Bearing in mind that, in the context of toy-sucking toddlers, the toy must be completely safe and nontoxic, make sure that the wood is of top quality and in first-class condition. Ideally, the plywood needs to be smooth-faced and compact, without filler or knots, and with the cut edges free of cavities. The wood to be turned must be straight-grained, free of

knots and splinters, and easy to work. We chose to use English beech because, as well as having all these qualities, it turns and works to a smooth, hard finish.

After you study the design templates (FIG. 4-3), take a tracing of the chassis base. Make sure that the curves and details are correct, and then pencil-press transfer the traced lines through to the working face of the piece of 3/8-inch plywood. The chassis needs to be 3 inches wide and 6 inches long, with a shaped front edge, curved corners, and a hole at front center for a pull cord. Once the design has been set out and checked, take the wood to the scroll saw and cut out the shape. Next drill out the cord hole with the 1/4-inch bit. Make good any damage with filler, and then use the graded sandpapers to rub the whole cutout down to a smooth-faced, slightly round-edged finish.

Creating the car body

When you have completed the chassis, put it to one side. Take the 6-inch length of 2-×-2½-inch wood—the piece for the car body—and set it down flat on the

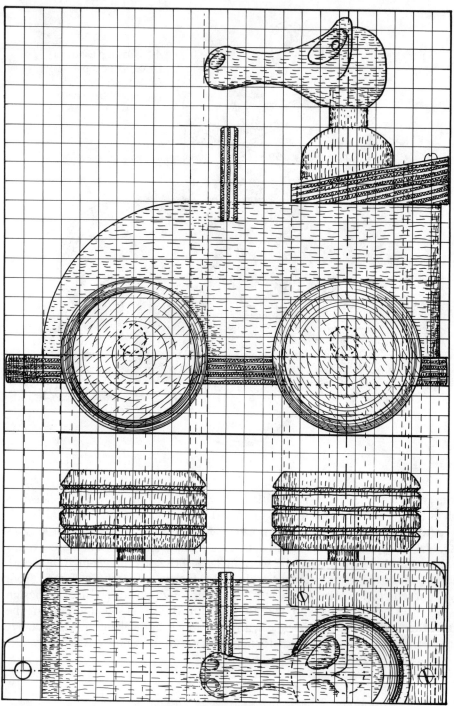

4-2 Working drawing. At a scale of four grid squares to 1 inch, the toy measures about 6 inches long, 5 inches wide, and 5 1/2 inches high from the ground to the top of the dinosaur's head.

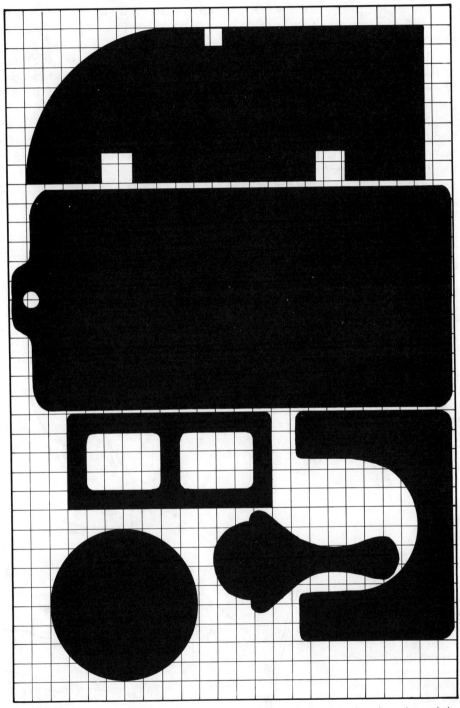

4-3 Design template. The scale is four grid squares to 1 inch. Note that the axles and the dinosaur's body are not shown.

workbench so that one of the two 6-×-2-inch side faces is uppermost. With a pencil, mark this face SIDE LEFT, and then mark the other faces TOP, FRONT, SIDE RIGHT, BOTTOM, and BACK, accordingly.

Use a pencil, ruler, compass, and square to set in all the details of the design of the body. For example, with the compass fixed to a radius of 2 inches, and working on the side of the wood marked SIDE LEFT, mark in the curve of the hood (FIG. 4-4, top left).

Now, bearing in mind that the channels need to run across the width of car body and be at right angles to the side faces, take a pencil, ruler, and square, and mark in the two axle channels on the bottom of the car body and the channel for the windshield on the top. Place the center of the windshield channel about $2^{1}/2$ inches from the front of the car, and the centers of the axle channels $2^{7}/8$ inches apart, with the front axle center about $1^{1}/4$ inch from the front of the hood. The $^{3}/8$-inch-diameter axles should be a well-contained, but easy-to-turn fit.

When you are happy with the way the wood has been set out, and are ready to cut the curve of the hood, place the wood with its side face uppermost on a cutting board. Using the straight saw, clear away the bulk of the waste with three or four well-placed cuts (FIG. 4-4, right). Run the cuts tangentially on the waste side

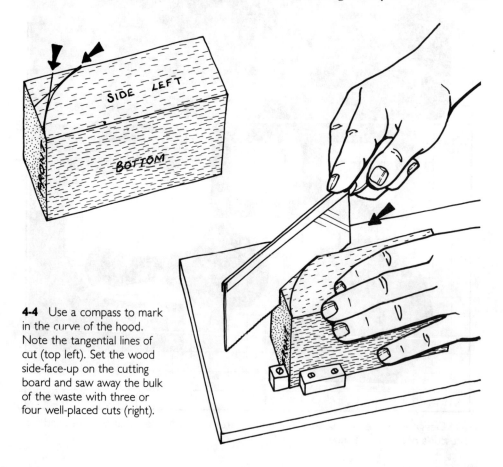

4-4 Use a compass to mark in the curve of the hood. Note the tangential lines of cut (top left). Set the wood side-face-up on the cutting board and saw away the bulk of the waste with three or four well-placed cuts (right).

of the drawn curved line. When you have cut away most of the waste with the saw, take the curve to a smooth finish with the chisel and sandpaper.

Before you cut the three channels, take the square and the chisel or knife and set the sides of the channels in with score marks. Once you have checked and double-checked that all is correct, secure the wood top-side-up in the muffled vise, and use the straight saw to establish the width and the depth of the windshield channel. Place the saw blade on the waste side of the scored lines, and run the cuts into the wood to a depth of $1/4$ inch. Take the $1/8$-inch-wide chisel and very carefully lower the waste to the depth of the initial saw cuts (FIG. 4-5). Don't try to chop the waste with a single thrust. Instead, work a series of little slicing cuts. To cut the axle channels, simply repeat the procedure, only this time, of course, the finished channels need to be slightly more than $3/8$ inch in width and depth.

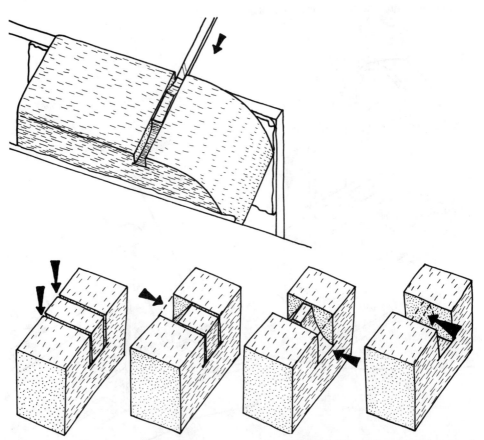

4-5 Set the car body in the muffled vise, make two parallel cuts to define the width and depth of the channel, and then use the $1/8$-inch-wide chisel to clear away the waste (top). To cut a channel, first set the depth and width with two saw cuts, then cut the waste from one side to the center, cut the waste from the other side to the center, and, finally, remove the last peak of waste to achieve a level base (bottom, left to right).

Dashing Dinosaur Driver **41**

Cutting the windshield

Have another look at the working drawings (FIG. 4-2), and see how the little wind-shield is cut and worked from 1/4-inch multicore plywood. Note the 1/4-inch measurement of the frame, and how all the corners, apart from the two at the bottom outer edge, are rounded. Using a pencil, ruler, and square, set out the shape of the windshield on a piece of 1/4-inch-thick multicore plywood. Shade in all the areas that need to be cut away. Then, using the drill with the 1/4-inch-diameter bit, run a pilot hole for the saw blade through each of the two enclosed window areas (FIG. 4-6, left).

Take the workpiece to the scroll saw, unhitch the saw blade, and pass it through one of the pilot holes. Fit and tension the blade, and then very carefully saw out the enclosed window of waste (FIG. 4-6, right). Repeat the procedure with the other window. When you cut the outside edge of the frame away from the waste, all you do is run the wood through the saw so that the moving blade is always presented with the line of next cut.

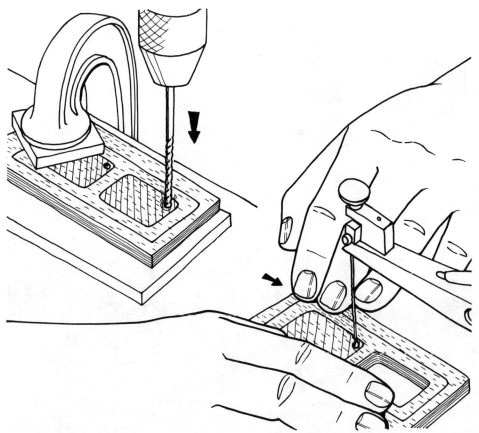

4-6 Run a pilot hole through each of the enclosed windows of waste (left). Refit and retension the blade and cut away the area of enclosed waste (right).

Finally, when you have what you consider to be a good windshield shape, take the fine-grade sandpaper and rub the cutout down to a smooth, slightly round-edged finish.

Working the bonnet or tonneau

Look again at the working drawing (FIG. 4-2) and note how the bonnet or tonneau (the piece around the back of the seat compartment) is cut and worked from 3/4-inch-thick multicore plywood so that it has a wedge shape. See the way the wedge angles down from a height of nearly 3/4 inch to a leading-edge thickness of no more than 1/4 inch.

Trace off the view from your working drawing and pencil-press transfer the shape through to your piece of 3/4-inch plywood. Label this face TOP and the other faces of the wood BOTTOM and SIDE accordingly.

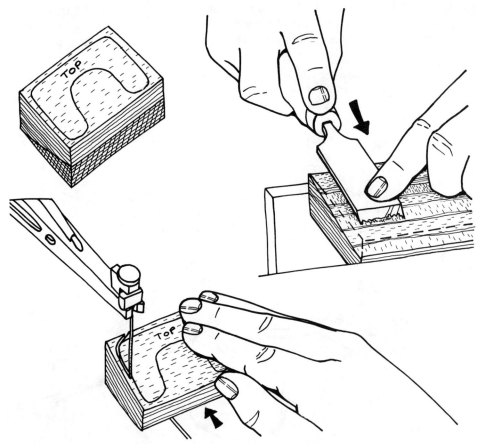

4-7 Mark the angle or wedge shape on the side of the wood (top left). Use a 1-inch-wide chisel to slice away the waste (right). With the drawn image uppermost, use the scroll saw to fret out the bonnet or tonneau shape, running the line of cut a little to the waste side of the drawn line (bottom left).

When you have drawn out the wraparound shape of the bonnet, and labeled the various faces of the wood, take a pencil and ruler and mark in on the two side faces the angle of the wedge-shaped profile (FIG. 4-7, top left). Now, set the wood top-side-down in the vise or against a bench stop, and use a chisel to swiftly slice down to the wedge line (FIG. 4-7, right). Don't try to chop off the waste with one great thrust, just go at it nice and easy, until you get down to the level of what will be the new bottom surface. Now flip the wood over so that the top—with the drawn image—is uppermost, and run the wood through the scroll saw to cut out the bonnet shape (FIG. 4-7, bottom left). Finally, take the graded sandpapers and rub the wedge-shaped bonnet down to a smooth-faced, round-edged, curve-cornered finish.

Turning the wheels and figure

Take your 20-inch length of 2¼-inch square, easy-to-turn wood, and check it over to make sure that it is free from knots, end splits, and rough grain. When you are happy that all is satisfactory, establish the end centerpoints by drawing in crossed diagonals with a pencil and ruler (FIG. 4-8, top). Now, remembering that wood-

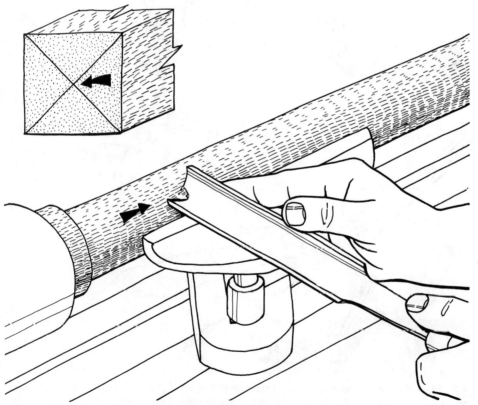

4-8 Draw crossed diagonals to establish the end centerpoints (top). Use a gouge to turn off the waste and to achieve a roughed-out cylinder (bottom).

turning can be dangerous, secure the wood in the lathe, position the tool rest, and organize the working area so that your tools are close to hand. Also make sure that you are suitably dressed and prepared.

After you have read through the safety checklist (see **lathe** in the glossary), turn on the power, and use the gouge of your choice—square-ended or round-nosed—to swiftly remove the bulk of the rough (FIG. 4-8, bottom). When you have turned the workpiece down to a smooth 2-inch-diameter cylinder, take the pencil ruler and dividers, and mark in on the spinning cylinder all the step-offs that go to make up the design of the wheels and the figure (FIG. 4-9, top). From left to right along the cylinder, allow about 5¹/₂ inches for chuck waste and for spares, then 2¹/₂ inches for the dinosaur's head, ¹/₂ inch for the neck, 3 inches for the body, another ¹/₄ inch for waste, and then alternate step-offs of 1 inch and ¹/₄ inch, for the wheels and the between-wheel waste. Reckon on making six wheels; then you can pick the best-matched four.

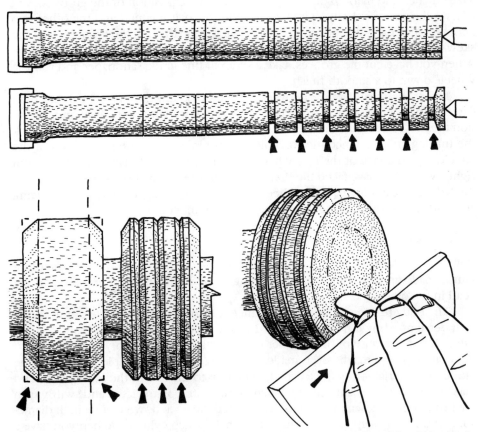

4-9 Working from left to right, mark in all the step-offs that go to make up the design (top). Next, sink all the ¹/₄-inch between-wheel waste areas (middle). Then cut away the little angle of waste from the sides of the wheels (bottom left). Use the skew chisel to cut the tire grooves (bottom center). Turn the face of the wheel down to a good finish (bottom right).

Note: The 20-inch length of wood allows a generous amount of extra wood, just in case you make a mess of one or other of the turnings and need to do a repeat. If you are an experienced, cost-cutting turner, you could get away with using a 16^1/$_2$-inch length of wood.

When you have marked in the step-offs, take the parting tool, and sink all the ^{1}/$_4$-inch-wide waste areas in to a depth of ^{1}/$_2$ inch. If all is well and as described, you should be left with a central core about 1 inch in diameter (FIG. 4-9, middle). Have a close look at the working drawings (FIG. 4-2, bottom), and see how each wheel is chamfered at the edges to give the effect of an angled tire or rim. Now, allowing for the chamfer to be about ^{3}/$_{16}$ inch wide and ^{3}/$_{16}$ inch deep, take the skew chisel or the parting tool, and cut away the little angle of waste from the sides of each of the wheels. The remaining tire width, meaning the face that comes into contact with the ground, should be about ^{5}/$_8$ inch wide (FIG. 4-9, bottom left).

Each wheel face is cut with three grooves to give a tread effect or pattern. Take a pencil and mark in on the spinning wood the position of the grooves. Aim to have the grooves about ^{1}/$_4$ inch apart—one groove at center and the other two about ^{1}/$_4$ inch each side of center. When you have marked in the grooves, take the skew chisel and cut out a little V to make each groove (FIG. 4-9, bottom center). When you have cut the grooves, take a scrap of fine-grade sandpaper and rub the wheels down to a smooth finish.

Lower the area of waste between the tailstock and the first wheel and then carefully part off the first wheel. Push the tailstock well out of the way, and reposition the tool rest so that it is set over the bed of the lathe and so that you can work the turning end-on. Once the workpiece is completely secure in the jaws of the chuck, turn the face of the first wheel down to a smooth finish (FIG. 4-9, bottom right). When you have faced the first wheel, put the tool rest back over the side of the lathe and carefully part the wheel off. Continue facing and parting off, facing and parting off, until all the wheels have been removed.

Turning the dinosaur figure

Have another look at the working drawings (FIG. 4-2), and note the way the dinosaur is made up from two separate turnings—the body and neck in one, and the head in the other.

The body turning is easy enough since it's no more than a little dome-ended cylinder topped by a neck stub. The head, on the other hand, is more complicated, if only because of the number of dips and curves. When you have studied the drawings, and maybe even made a working model with a piece of Plasticine modeling material, bring the tailstock center up to the end of the body piece, and make sure that all is secure and well-centered. Switch on the lathe and swiftly turn the head step-off down to a 1^1/$_2$-inch diameter, the neck down to a ^{1}/$_2$-inch diameter, and the body step-off down to a smooth 1^1/$_4$-inch cylinder. When you have a clear understanding of just how the forms need to be worked, take a pencil and mark in, on the spinning wood, the position of all the hills and valleys that make up the shape of the head and body. So, for example, the distance from the end of

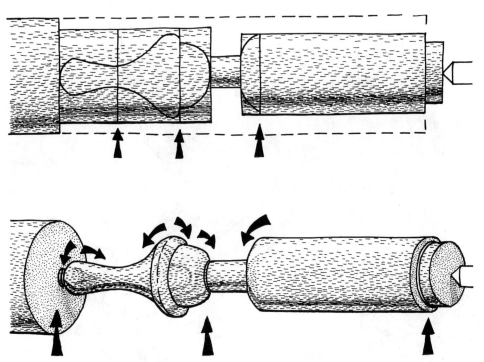

4-10 Pencil in all the design step-offs and try to visualize the design (top). Use the skew chisel to lower the waste wood, working with the grain down towards the valleys (bottom).

the round snout to the top of the eye ridge is about 2 inches, the distance from the eye ridge to the back of the head is $1/2$ inch, the narrow part of the snout occurs about 1 inch along from the end of the snout, and so on. Study your designs and the turning and try to visualize the finished design as being hidden just below the surface of the wood (FIG. 4-10, top).

Take the tool of your choice—you might use a skew chisel or perhaps a small round-nosed gouge—and start by sinking a number of depth guides. You'll need one for the snout valley, one to define the diameter of the back of the head, and one between the back of the head and what will be the top of the shoulders.

Take the skew chisel, and very carefully cut back the waste. Gradually lower the wood down to the valleys and define the curves until the form takes shape (FIG. 4-10, bottom). Finally, rub the work down to a good finish and part off. When you are parting off, dish the base slightly to ensure that the dinosaur can stand upright.

Whittling the head

Look at the working drawing again to see how to complete the dinosaur's face. The initial turning needs to be whittled and worked with both the knife and the spoon gouge. Quarter the turning by eye, and, with a pencil, and label the quarters TOP LEFT, TOP RIGHT, BOTTOM LEFT, and BOTTOM RIGHT (FIG. 4-11, top left).

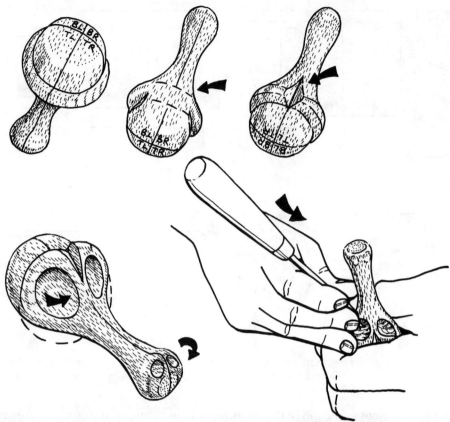

4-11 Quarter the turning by eye and label the quarters with a pencil (top left). Carefully cut away the rim on the bottom left and the bottom right areas (top middle). Cut a V-shaped nick out of the rim at the center of the top to form the two eye brows (top right). Use the little spoon gouge to scoop out the waste to create the eye sockets and the nostril holes (bottom).

Now, carefully supporting the turning bottom-side-up in your noncarving hand, take the knife and, much as you might pare an apple, carefully cut away the rim on the bottom left and bottom right quarters (FIG. 4-11, top center). Whittle away the whole of the rim on the underside, until the back of the head runs in a smooth curve through to the cheek and snout. Next, hold the head top side up, then take the knife, and cut a V-shaped nick out of the rim at top center (FIG. 4-11, top right). Gradually lower the V and reshape the rim left and right, until you form two quite separate eyebrows.

Mark in the position of the eye sockets. Take the little spoon gouge and carefully scoop out the waste wood to make the deep sharp-edged eye socket holes (FIG. 4-11, bottom right). Work one hole, and then the other, and back to the first hole, until you have two well-matched sockets. Repeat the procedure on a smaller scale for the two nostril holes (FIG. 4-11, bottom left). Finally, take a scrap of fine-grade sandpaper and rub the wood down to a smooth finish.

Drilling the holes

Before you start painting, bore out the various holes. The neck stub hole is simple enough—just drill a 3/8-inch-diameter hole in the underside of the head and trim the neck stub to a push fit. The axle holes are a little more complicated, but only because they are set off-center. Look at the working drawings (FIG. 4-2), and see how the edge of the 3/8-inch-diameter axle hole cuts through the centerpoint of the wheel. To establish the position of the axle hole centers, set the compass to a radius of 3/16 inch, spike the compass point on the wheel center, and draw a circle. The axle hole centerpoint can be set at any point along the circumference of this circle (FIG. 4-13, bottom right). Drill the four holes to a depth of about 1/2 inch.

Finally, run screw-fixing holes through the chassis base and through the tonneau, and bore out the 1 1/2-inch-diameter seat hole. *Note:* If your finished dinosaur body happens to be larger than 1 1/4 inches in diameter—don't forget to allow for paint thickness—then all you do is adjust the size of seat hole to fit.

Painting

Once you cut the two axles to length, you should have eleven components—four wheels, two axle rods, the chassis slab, the car body, the windshield, the bonnet or tonneau, and the dinosaur—all drilled, sanded, and ready to be painted. *Note:* Leave the axles unpainted.

This project is easy to paint, because apart from a small amount of detail on the head, and the two headlight circles, the pieces need no more than a straightforward allover coat (FIG. 4-12). Start by cleaning up all the dust and debris; then move to the area you have set aside for painting. Cover the work surface with newspaper, rig up a drying line or a rack, and generally arrange all the brushes and paints so that they are close at hand. Paint the chassis base yellow, the body dark blue, the wheels, bonnet, and windshield red, the headlights yellow, and the dinosaur green. Lay on several coats—don't forget to sand in between layers until the colors are dense and even. When the dinosaur is dry, paint the eye sockets white, and dot in the nostrils and the eye pupils with black paint.

Putting together and finishing

With the two parts well aligned, start by screw-fixing the chassis base from the underside into the body of the car (FIG. 4-13). Set the screws at the back, front, and sides so that they are well clear of the axle channels and the seat hole. Glue the windshield in its channel, and screw-fix the bonnet in position on the topside of the car body. Take the two axles, cut "glue ooze" slots (FIG. 4-13, top right), slide the axles through the channels, dab a little glue over the slotted ends, and push them home into the wheel holes. Allowing a 1/16-inch, easy-running gap between the side of the chassis and the inside face of the wheel, set the wheels on the axles so that they match—wheels up and axles down.

Touch up any scuff marks, and give the whole toy a couple of coats of clear varnish. Finally, when the varnish is dry, fix the pull-cord with a screw-eye, and the car is ready for its first wibble-wobble test drive.

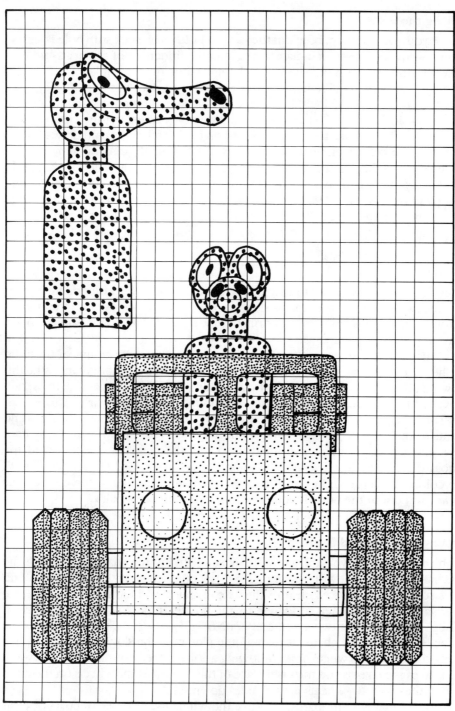

4-12 Painting grid.

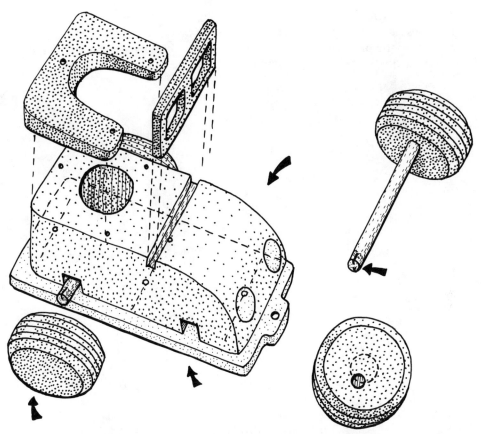

4-13 Establish the axle hole centers by drawing a 3/8-inch-diameter circle on the wheels. The axle holes must occur on the circumference of the drawn circle (bottom right). Screw the chassis from the underside into the body block. Glue the windscreen into its channel. Screw-fix the bonnet (tonneau) in position. Cut and slot the axles and slide them through the channels. Glue the wheels onto the axle so that they are both in the same position (left).

Hints

- Give the scroll saw cutting table a wax polishing just prior to use. The resulting friction-free surface makes for easy movement of the wood that you are sawing.
- As with most of the projects, if you can only afford to buy one sheet of plywood, go for the 1/4-inch thickness and stick layers together to make thicker laminations.
- Working all the turnings from the same section wood is a bit wasteful because you will be turning down to several different diameters. Of course, if you use two pieces of wood—one for the wheels and one for the dinosaur—you will have twice as much headstock and tailstock waste and twice as much to rough out! Think about which option is better for you.

- Always allow for paint buildup. For example, since the total windshield thickness is $1/4$ inch plus at least two coats of paint, then either you have to sand back the paint prior to gluing, or you have to make the body channel just a fraction wider than $1/4$ inch to allow for the thickness of paint.

5

Dinosaur Movie Stars

THIS APATOSAURUS and allosaurus are American movie stars who like nothing better than to perform in front of an audience. They exist for the moment when the handle is turned and they are set into motion. The only trouble is, that just like one or two real-life movie stars—we won't mention any names—they both have an eating problem. Do they eat too much? Or are they messy? Or do they have a yen for exotic, impossible-to-obtain dishes? Not exactly. The truth is, that while the apatosaurus—pronounced a-pat-oh-saw-rus—likes eating freshly gathered water plants, the allosaurus—al-oh-saw-rus—likes eating freshly gathered water-plant eaters! Poor old Apatosaurus, as soon as his back is turned and he is happily crunching and munching his way through a nice juicy lunch of water weeds, Allosaurus tries to take a bite of his favorite food—namely Apatosaurus. In fact—we hope you are ready for this rather unpleasant detail—many an apatosaurus skeleton has been found with allosaurus teeth marks on the tail bones!

Tools and materials
- A sheet of best-quality, white-faced, $1/4$-inch-thick multicore plywood at 36×36 inches, for the nine layers that make up the box body, the animals, and all the moving parts, with a generous amount to spare
- An 18-inch length of $1/4$-inch-diameter dowel for all the rods and pivots, allowing for spare and cutting waste
- Four 3-inch-long, thin tension springs (or you might use heavy-duty elastic bands)
- Seven small brass screw-eyes
- A $1 1/4$-inch-diameter, colored wooden bead for the turn-handle knob
- A small quantity of Super Glue fast-drying adhesive
- A try square
- A pencil, ruler, and compass
- A large sheet of workout paper
- A large sheet of tracing paper

- A large roll of double-sided tape
- A large, straight, flat-bladed saw
- An electric scroll saw (we use a Hegner)
- A press drill with a ¼-inch-diameter bit
- A pack of graded sandpapers
- A small amount of two-tube wood filler
- Acrylic paints in light, medium, and dark green; yellow; orange; red; pale blue; white; and black
- A can of clear, high-shine varnish
- A couple of brushes—one broad and one fine-point

Looking and planning

This dinosaur movie machine (FIG. 5-1) is a beautiful, fun, classic toy. With roots that go way back to nineteenth-century playthings like "Penny Peeps" and "What the Butler Saw," and one or two other penny movie machines, toys of this type are still amazingly popular with kids. Hang it on the wall, slowly turn the handle, and watch the little picture come alive—wonderful! As you turn the handle, the apatosaurus moves his head, legs, and tail, and the allosaurus snaps his mouth open and shut, and blinks his eye. You might think that children would soon get bored with the simple, repetitive movements, but they don't. Kids enjoy toys of

5-1   Dinosaur Movie Stars—Turn the handle to start the action.

this character precisely because they are so predictable and repetitious. The tots get a lot of pleasure from being in control and knowing just what is going to happen when they turn the handle.

Have a good, long, in-depth look at the working drawings (FIG. 5-2) and the design templates (FIGS. 5-3 and 5-4), and see how the toy is made up of ten layers of 1/4-inch-thick plywood—two facade, or proscenium, foliage layers, a single spacer between the back of the facade and the box, the painted scene layer, and the six layers that go to make up the actual box. The working parts are fixed to the back of the painted scene and are contained and protected by the box. Consider how the basic lever, cam, and spring movement is set in motion by the turn-handle cam. The revolving cam lifts the head lever, which opens and closes the mouth. Then the cam goes on to flip against the long-armed H, moving it backwards and forwards, which in turn sets the apatosaurus's head and tail moving up and down. And so the movement continues for as long as someone turns the handle.

Although at first sight the movement might look to be complicated, it is, in fact, relatively simple. The slender springs pull the levers back into place, the weight of the large head causes the long lever to fall down and come to rest against its stop, and so on. If you do have any doubts as to how the various parts fit together and are set into motion, make a cardboard and pin prototype before you start. This way you can actually see how the levers, pivots, and cam all work and relate one to another before you put tool to wood. Finally, draw the design up to full size.

Setting out the boards

Once you have sorted out in your own mind precisely how the movie toy works and operates, take a pencil and ruler, and mark the 36-×-36-inch sheet of plywood so that it is divided into twelve identical 9-×-12-inch boards (FIG. 5-5, top left). Make sure the grid is set square and that all corners are at right angles; then take the large saw and very carefully slice the wood down into the twelve component sheets. Run the saw through the wood so that the blade is at right angles, and work at a nice, easy, relaxed pace so as not to rip or tear the grain.

Select the best ten boards and put the other two to one side for spares or for another project. Group the ten boards so that you have two stacks—one with eight boards and the other with two. Take the double-sided tape and sandwich the plywood layers together. Set the tape within 1 inch of the edge of the board. You should now have two plywood sandwiches, each measuring 9×12 inches—one 1/2 inch and the other 2 inches thick (FIG. 5-5, top right). When you are happy with your groups, take the two-board stack and use a pencil, ruler, try square, and compass to set all four corners out with clean, 1-inch-radius curves (FIG. 5-5, bottom). Take the eight-board stack, reduce the overall size to 8×11 inches and repeat the corner radius-curve procedure.

Fretting out the boards

When you have both stacks clearly and crisply marked with smooth radius-curve corners, set to work on the scroll saw, cutting out all the straight lines and curves

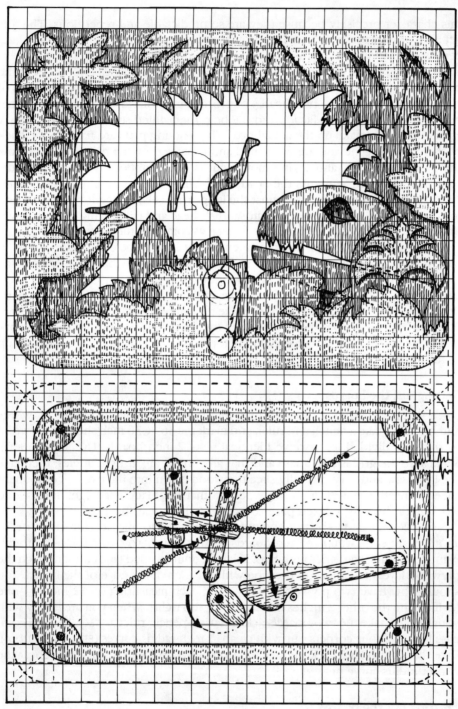

5-2 Working drawings. The scale is two grid squares to 1 inch. The first and second facade layers, plus the dinosaurs and the handle (top); looking in from the back of the box to see the moving parts (bottom). The arrows indicate direction of movement.

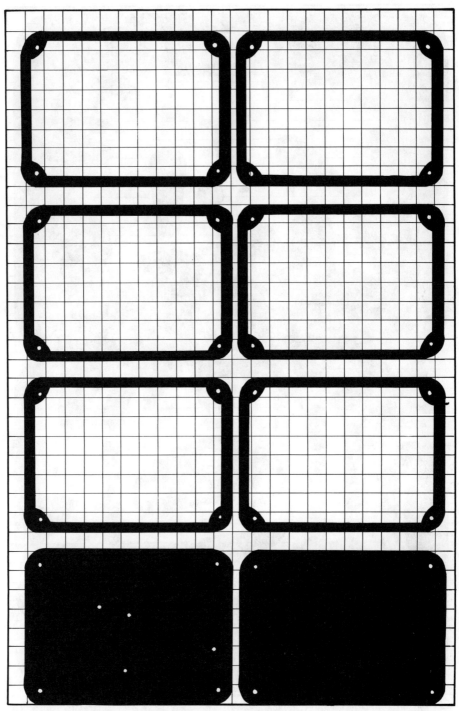

5-3 Design templates (not to scale) for the five box layers, the spacer between the facades and the box, and the front and back box boards.

5-4 Design templates for the two facade layers. The scale is two grid squares to 1 inch. The second facade layer consists of foliage, the apatosaurus, and the parts for the handle (top); the first facade layer has foliage, the allosaurus, the levers, and the cams (bottom).

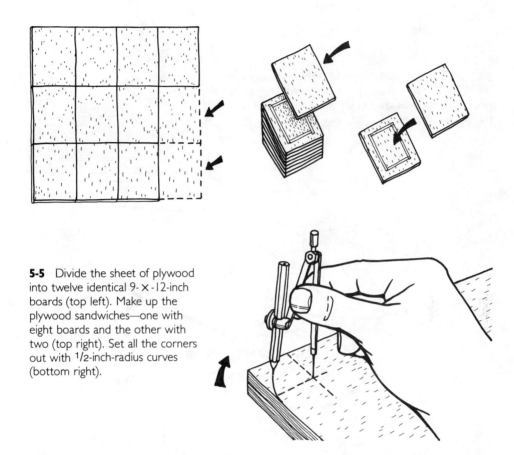

5-5 Divide the sheet of plywood into twelve identical 9- × -12-inch boards (top left). Make up the plywood sandwiches—one with eight boards and the other with two (top right). Set all the corners out with 1/2-inch-radius curves (bottom right).

that make up the board shape. With the blade well-tensioned and the saw-table surface clean and polished, switch on the power and run the workpiece through the saw. Bearing in mind that straight lines and part-circle curves are much more difficult to cut than multicurved profiles, work at an easy pace, all the while manipulating the wood so that the line of cut is slightly to the waste side of the drawn line, and so that the moving blade is presented with the line of next cut in a timely manner. The process is easy enough, as long as you make allowances for saw-blade "wander" and keep an eye on the pace of the wood as it moves forward. If you are a beginner, do a tryout with scrap until you get comfortable with such factors as blade wander and speed. Don't worry if you make a mess of the scrap, just be comforted by the fact that practice makes perfect.

When you have cleared away the waste, take the eight-board stack and use the pencil, ruler, and compass to establish the inside-box shape. With the border thickness set out at 1/2 inch, fix the compass at a radius of 1 inch, and then, one corner at a time, spike the point on the outer curve and scribe the arc that makes up the inside-box corner. Fix the centerpoints of the four dowel rods by measuring in about 5/8 inch from each outer corner curve. Then put the 1/4-inch- diameter bit in the drill and sink the four corner holes right through the eight-stack sandwich (FIG. 5-6, top).

Dinosaur Movie Stars **59**

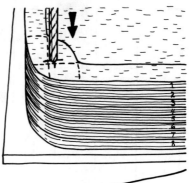

5-6 Set the ¼-inch-diameter bit in the drill and run the four corner holes through the eight-layer stack (top). Use the scroll saw to clear away the area of central waste (bottom).

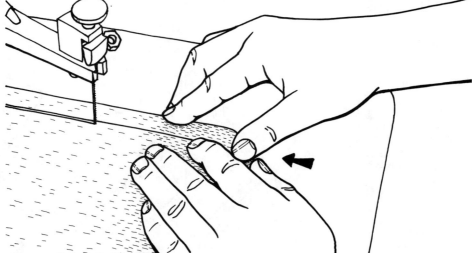

Number the layers from 1 to 8, so that the top background scene board is numbered 1. Remove boards 2 and 8, rebuild the stack, and then run a ¼-inch-diameter pilot hole through the six-board stack and use the scroll saw to clear away the central waste area (FIG. 5-6, bottom). Finally, rub all cut edges down to a smooth finish.

Fretting out the facade boards and moving parts

You should now have two large 9-×-12-inch facade boards; the six-layer 8-×-11-inch frame box, still stuck together with the double-sided tape, but with the center cut away and the corner holes bored through; and two 8-×-11-inch box boards complete with corner holes. Drill the pivot holes in the front of box board 2—two pivot holes for the apatosaurus, one for the allosaurus, and one for the handle. Take the eight 8-×-11-inch boards, peel away all the sticky tape, and rebuild the stack in the numbered sequence. When you are done, cut four 2¼-inch-long, ¼-inch-diameter dowels and tap them for a tight fit through the corner holes so that the box is contained and lidded.

When you have built the box, put it to one side, and take up the two large 9-×-12-inch facade boards. Remove the tape. Now trace off the facade foliage designs (FIG. 5-4), and carefully pencil-press transfer the traced lines through to the wood. Make sure, from board to board, that the turn-handle pivot holes are precisely placed in relationship to each other and to the moving parts.

Go back to the scroll saw and set to work fretting out the profile of the facade boards. Proceed just as before, only this time you can be a bit more relaxed—it doesn't matter too much if the lines of cut wander away from the drawn line. Of course, you do have to make sure that the fern or bush at the lower right is large enough to mask the pivot hole for the allosaurus head. Repeat the drawing and sawing procedure with all the moving parts—the levers, the cams, the dinosaurs, and so on.

Finally, when you have cut out all the component parts, run the 1/4-inch drill bit through all pivot hole centers, repair damage with the filler, and rub all faces and cut edges down with the graded sandpapers.

Painting

When you have worked all the pieces that make up the design, do a trial assembly, and make sure that the fit and order of the various components is correct. Use a pencil to establish the eye when the head is raised and lowered. If you have made a mistake with a profile or with the position of a drill hole or whatever, now is the time to put things right. When you are happy that all is as it should be, move to the area that you have set aside for painting.

Pin the designs and working drawings up on the wall, cover the work surface with newspaper, and generally sort out what needs to be painted and what needs to be left plain. You need to paint the first and second facade boards, the front scene board, the allosaurus head, the handle, and the apatosaurus. Put everything else to one side. Have a look at the painting grids (FIGS. 5-7 and 5-8) and working drawings and make a note of colors. See how the handle is bright red, the first facade pieces are worked in various shades of light green, the second facade board is dark green, the large dinosaur's head is bright red with white and black details, and the small dinosaur is bright yellow. Look at the scene board on the front of the box (FIG. 5-8), and note how the sand is yellow-orange, the water light blue, the palm tree tops medium green, the sky off-white, and so on. Sort out your chosen colors and make sure that they are well stirred before you use them.

Start by tracing and pencil-press transferring the scene through to the front face of box board 2. Now, beginning with the large areas, lay the colors on in smooth, even coats. If you need to give a piece a second coat, then let the paint dry and give it a swift rubdown with sandpaper between coats. Trace the design details onto the first facade pieces and onto the large dinosaur's head. And so you continue, gradually blocking in the design areas and working towards the smaller details. Finally, when you are pleased with the imagery and the overall effect, give all the components—both painted and plain—a couple of coats of thin, clear varnish and put them to one side to dry.

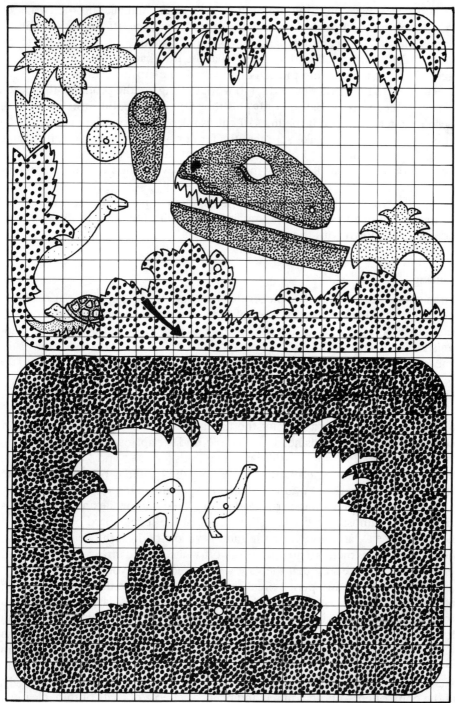

5-7 Painting grid for the first facade (top) and the second facade (bottom). See the painting grid color code in the glossary. The scale is two grid squares to I inch.

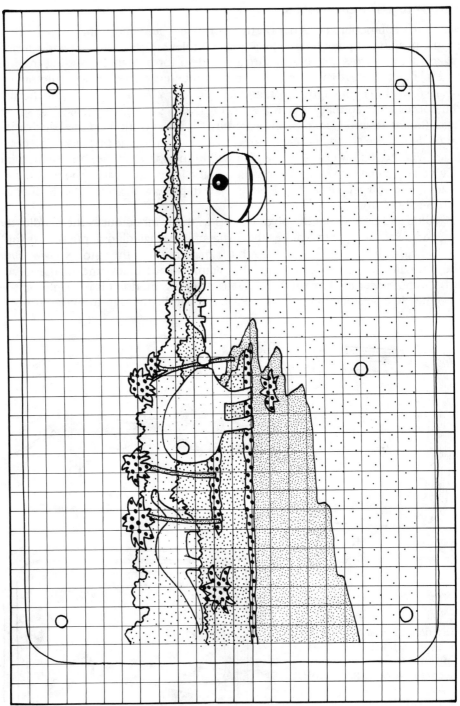

5-8 Painting grid for the scene board at the front of the box. See the painting grid color code in the glossary. The scale is three grid squares to 1 inch.

Putting together and finishing

Set all the component parts out on the workbench and check them over. Check on the position of pivot holes, check that all holes are clear of paint and varnish, make sure all pivots are an easy-turn fit, and so forth. Start by putting the box together. Set the box layers in the correct numbered sequence, with the picture board (board 2) being uppermost, and tap the four $2^1/_4$-inch dowel pins through the corner holes so that $^1/_4$ inch is showing (FIG. 5-9, top). Next, take the spacer layer (board 1), and glue, pin, and carefully fix it in position on the back of the large, dark-green second facade board, and temporary fix the first facade pieces in place. Fix the red lower jaw in position within the spacer frame, bearing in mind that you might have to check the position of the lower jaw against the pivoted red head before you get it just right. Hold the jaw in place with only a couple of brads (FIG. 5-9, bottom).

Glue and position all the pivot dowels in the front cutouts—the handle, the large red head, and the two pieces that make up the small dinosaur (FIG. 5-10, top). Paint the on-view dowel ends to match the main body of the cutouts. Now, slide the dinosaur dowel pivots through the picture board holes, and fit the facade boards and spacer in place on the box (FIG. 5-10). Again, don't use the glue at this stage just in case something is amiss. Push the handle through from the front.

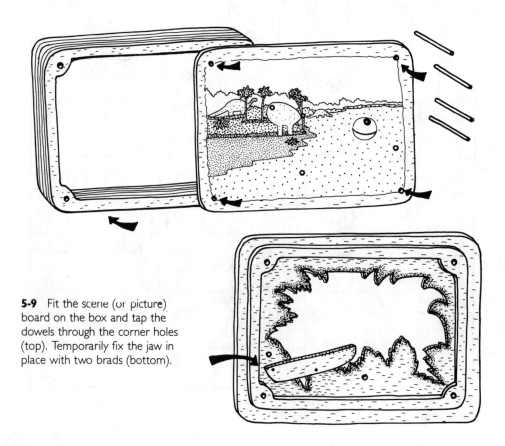

5-9 Fit the scene (or picture) board on the box and tap the dowels through the corner holes (top). Temporarily fix the jaw in place with two brads (bottom).

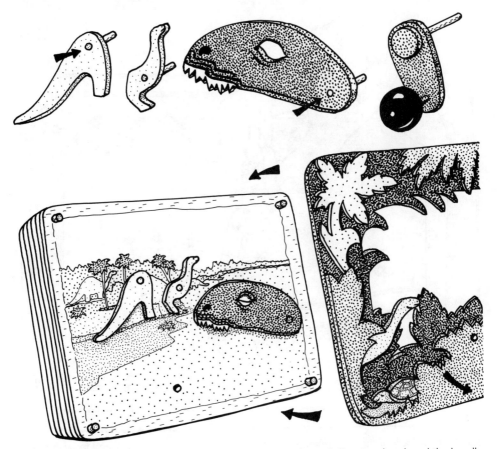

5-10 Glue the dowels into the cutouts: the apatosaurus, the red allosaurus head, and the handle (top). Fit the apatosaurus and the allosaurus-head dowels through the picture board, and position the spacer and facades on the four dowel knobs (bottom).

Turn the box over so that you can see the inside, and be ready with the various small parts that make the lever mechanism. Start by sliding the cam on the turn-pivot dowel so that it is hard up against the back of the picture board. Adjust the cam to allow for smooth and easy movement; then fix it in position with a small dab of Super Glue. Slide the long lift lever in place on the large head dowel. Adjust the lever so that the turning cam lifts the top of the dinosaur's head to the correct height, and again glue-tack it in position. Next, slide the two levers on the pivots that operate the small dinosaur's head and tail, link the uprights with the cross bar and the screw eyes (FIG. 5-11), and again tack with glue to hold the whole thing in place. Check the movement by turning the pivot handle in a counter-clockwise direction. If all is well, the cam should lift the red head lever, and flip against the long yellow dinosaur lever. Again, you might need to make adjustments until everything works just right. When you have what you consider to be a good smooth movement, fit the springs and the screw eyes so that after each revolution of the turn-handle the levers are pulled back into place. Finally, make good

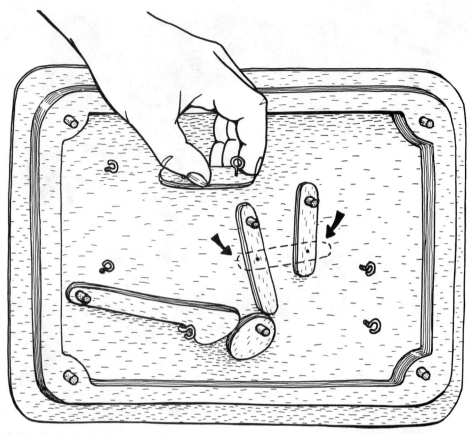

5-11 At the back of the box, link the two dinosaur levers with a cross bar and fix with screw-eyes to make an H shape.

all the joint and pivot fixings by adding more glue, pop the back lid on the box, glue the first facade in place, and the toy is ready to be hung on the wall.

Hints

- Take care when you do the sawing. If you are a beginner, spend time having a trial run on scrap wood. Draw out a few circles, and see if you can keep to within 1/16 inch of the waste side of the drawn line.
- For a super-smooth movement, rub a little wax polish on all mating moving surfaces.
- You will need to rub down all pivots slightly with sandpaper so that they are an easy-turn fit in 1/4-inch-diameter holes.
- If you don't want to buy tension springs, you could use heavy-duty elastic bands.
- You could make the box shallower, with four 1/4-inch-thick sheets of plywood.
- Keep the relatively large pieces of inside-box waste for other projects.

6

Terry the Pteranodon Test Pilot

Is IT A BIRD? Is it a plane? No, it's Terry the pteranodon test pilot, gracefully gliding around on eddies of warm air. Now, just to get the record straight, dinosaurs never flew, and a pteranodon is not, strictly speaking, a dinosaur. Rather, the pteranodon—pronounced ter-an-oh-don and belonging to a group known as pterosaurs—is a close reptile cousin of the dinosaur.

As Terry skillfully uses the rising currents of warm air to gain height, she smiles as she considers how long it took *Homo sapiens* to become airborne. As she remembers, humans had long dreamt of flying. The Emperor Shun in ancient China had tried flying, and then Leonardo da Vinci, and Montgolfier, and Otto von Lilenthal, and many others. But as we all know, it wasn't until 1903, when the American Wright brothers first started flying around, that people finally got their feet off the ground.

Terry swoops, performs a triple back flip beak-dive, scoops up a fish, and then rises on another current of air. She muses about her great-crested grandpappy, Pteranodon I, who had a record-breaking wingspan of 22 feet when he flew around quite happily more than 70 million years ago. Makes you think, doesn't it?

Tools and materials

- A sheet of best-quality, white-faced, 1/8-inch-thick multicore plywood, about 12×12 inches
- Three or four colored wooden beads of various sizes, for the counterbalance bob
- A pencil and ruler
- A sheet of workout paper
- A sheet of tracing paper
- A roll of double-sided tape

- A fretsaw and a pack of spare blades
- A bird's-mouth cutting board with a table clamp to fit
- A hand drill with a $1/16$-inch-diameter bit
- A pack of graded sandpapers
- Acrylic paints in dark green, light green, red, yellow, white, and black
- A small quantity of clear, high-shine varnish
- A couple of paint brushes—one broad and one fine-point
- A ball of strong, fine twine for the harness
- A needle to fit the twine that is small enough to pass through a $1/16$-inch-diameter hole

Looking and planning

When we first saw reference to a wooden butterfly toy in a magazine from the 1930s, the idea of creating a "delicate, easy-to-make mobile" out of wood didn't sound too promising. But when we eventually put together our first prototype from plywood, pins, and string, we were pleasantly surprised.

This toy has a beautiful action, it is delicate, it is easy to make and modify, and it is both intriguing and ingenious. Have a look at the project picture (FIG. 6-1) and the working drawings (FIG. 6-2), and see how the body of the pteranodon counterbalances the wings, while in turn, the body is counterbalanced by its own adjustable bob weight. Note the position of all the twine holes, and the way the harness cords are threaded through both the wings and the whiffletree, or balance beam. You might say that this project hinges, both literally and metaphorically, on all the forms, holes, and cords being precisely and nicely worked. However, because the project uses thin, $1/8$-inch-thick plywood (even thinner if you can find it), the actual working techniques—the sawing and drilling—can be managed with a minimum of expertise. All in all, this project is a really good tryout for beginners who have a restricted work space and a minimal toolkit.

Setting out the design and first cuts

When you have studied the working drawings (FIG. 6-2) and have a clear understanding of how the toy needs to be made and put together, stop awhile and consider how you might modify the design. For example, you could make a toy twice the size. Or have a whole family of pteranodons at graded sizes. Or then again, maybe you want to change the imagery and have a feathered archaeopteryx, an enormous Quetzalcoatl, or a beaked rhamphorhynchus. All such points need to be considered before you put tool to wood.

Once you have decided just how you want the project to be, draw the design (FIG. 6-3) out to full size, make a tracing of the profiles and drill holes, and then pencil-press transfer the traced lines through to the $1/8$-inch plywood. Make sure that all hole centerpoints are clearly and precisely established.

When you are happy with the way the shapes are set out, check that the bird's-mouth cutting board is securely clamped so that the V overhangs the edge of the bench (FIG. 6-4, top), make sure the fretsaw blade is nicely tensioned in the frame, and then cut the wood down into easy-to-handle shapes. Don't try at this

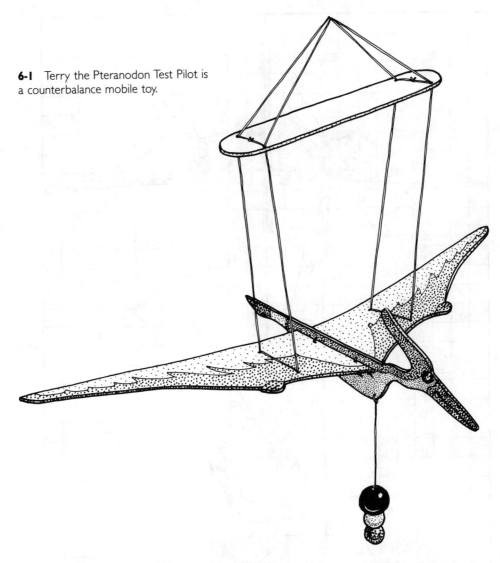

6-1 Terry the Pteranodon Test Pilot is a counterbalance mobile toy.

stage to cut up to the drawn line, just settle for swiftly zooming around the drawn shapes so that the line of cut is about ¼ inch to the waste side of the drawn line (FIG. 6-4, bottom).

Fretting and drilling

Take the two roughed-out wings, set them one on top of another so that the best drawn image is uppermost, and then sandwich them together with strips of double-sided tape (FIG. 6-5, top). Then carefully fret out the forms. As you are working, try not to twist the blade or apply too much pressure. Work at an even pace, all the while making sure that you cut on the waste side of the drawn lines and

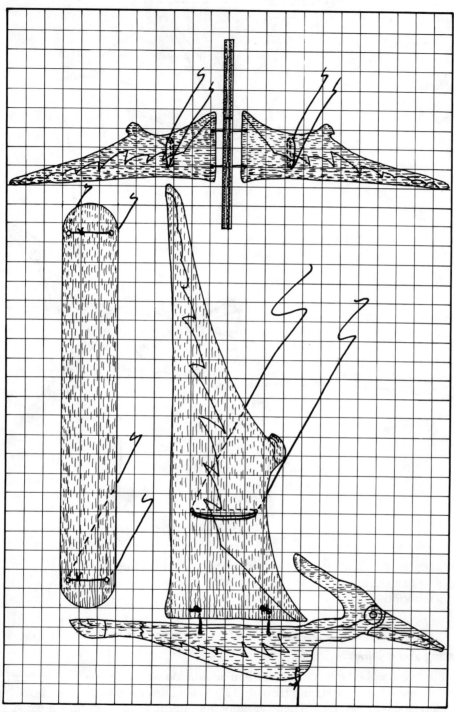

6-2 Working drawings. Note how the strings are attached to the different parts of the mobile. The top portion is not drawn to scale; at the bottom, the scale is about two grid squares to 1 inch.

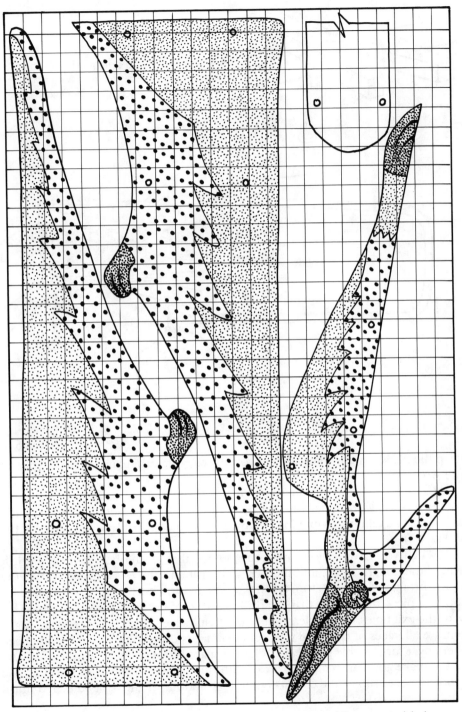

6-3 Design template and painting grid. The scale is about three grid squares to 1 inch.

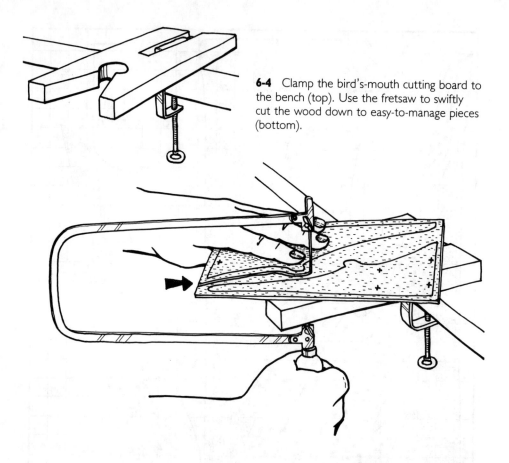

6-4 Clamp the bird's-mouth cutting board to the bench (top). Use the fretsaw to swiftly cut the wood down to easy-to-manage pieces (bottom).

keep the blade at right angles to the working face. Be careful not to rip or splinter the wood.

Using a bird's-mouth fretsaw table is easy enough, as long as the board is clamped to the work surface so that the V-notch extends beyond the surface, and as long as you minimize vibration by sawing as near as possible to the vertex of the V (FIG. 6-5).

When you have cut out the forms, check that all the hole centers are just where they ought to be, and then use the drill and the 1/16-inch bit to run the holes through the wood (FIG. 6-6, top). As you are drilling, place the workpiece on top of a piece of scrap so that the drill-exit face of the wood is supported. This way, the exit holes will be clean-cut rather than ragged. Ease the two wings apart, remove all traces of tape, and then set the cutouts down on the bench and check them over for possible problems. When you are happy with the profiles and the holes, make good any damaged areas with filler. Then take a scrap of fine-grade sandpaper and rub all the cutouts down to a smooth, slightly round-edged finish (FIG. 6-6, bottom).

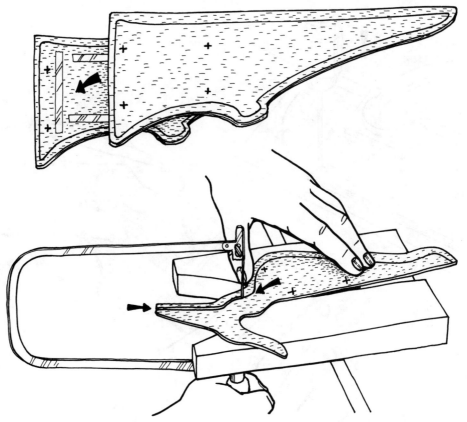

6-5 Sandwich the two rough-cut wing shapes together with straps of double-sided tape (top). To prevent vibration, saw as close as possible to the vertex of the V in the cutting board (bottom).

Painting

You should have four profiles in all—the two identical wings, the body piece, and the long round-ended strip that serves as the cross beam, sometimes called a whiffletree. When you are happy that all is correct, wipe away the dust, clear up the debris, and move to the area you have set aside for painting.

After you set out all the paints and materials, have a look at the painting grid (FIG. 6-3), and note how all sides of the work have to be painted. Then trace off the main color block lines and transfer them through to the profiles. When you start painting, paint all the plywood edges first, then the faces, and then the smaller areas of pattern and design color. Working in this way, you don't have to worry about drying racks and such, because by the time you have painted the edges and then one face, the edges will be dry enough to hold so that you can paint the other face. And so you continue, painting the top of the body and the leading edges of the wings dark green, the bottom of the body and the trailing edges of

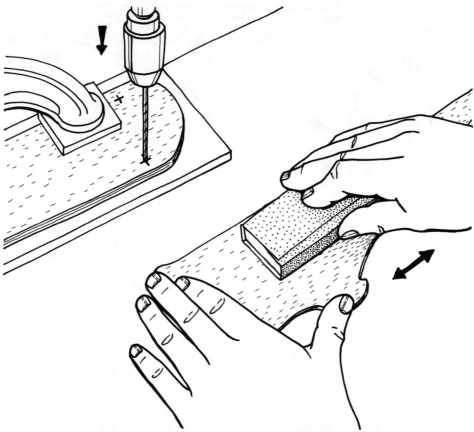

6-6 Use the drill and the 1/16-inch-diameter bit to run all the string holes through the wood (top). Use a block and fine-grade sandpaper to rub all the surfaces to a smooth finish (bottom).

the wings light green, the whiffletree white, and so on. If you need more than one coat to cover, don't forget to give the work a light sanding between coats. When you have painted the main areas of base color, take the fine-point brush and paint in all the small details—the eyes with the yellow pupils, red rims, and white shine, and the black feet, beak, and hands.

When you have what you consider is a strong, well-painted image, clear the holes of paint, wait a while for the paint to dry thoroughly, and then give the whole workpiece a couple of coats of clear varnish. Make sure that all holes are kept clear of paint and varnish.

Stringing up

Have another long, careful look at the project picture (FIG. 6-1) and the working drawings (FIG. 6-2), and note how the pteranodon needs to be threaded up. The whiffletree is hung from the ceiling, the wings are strung and knotted on either side of the body and suspended from the whiffletree, and then the whole arrangement is given its dynamic flapping form by the counterbalance bob weight hung from the underside of the body. Although the arrangement of the various strings and knots is pretty straightforward, the fine adjustment of the bob weight is more than a little bit difficult. If the bob is too heavy, the wing tips flip right up so that they touch each other, and if the bob is too light, then the wing tips sag down and the body goes up. The frustrating thing is, that while you try the various combinations of bead weight, the strings get tangled! Ask a friend to help.

Start by knotting the wings and the body together. Use a repeated double-twisted overhand knot until the knot is built up enough to prevent the cord from passing back through the hole (FIG. 6-7, left). First thread the needle and tie a knot in the end of the twine, then run the needle up from the underside of the wing, through the wing hole, through a body hole, down through the other wing hole,

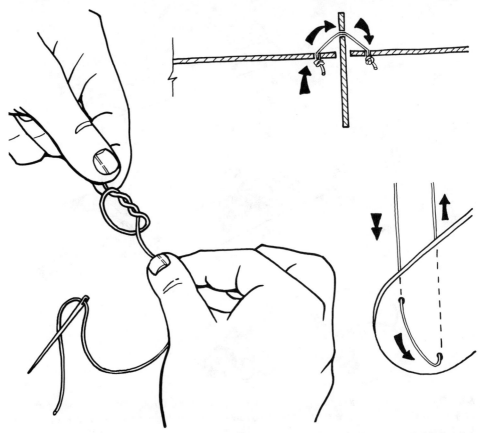

6-7 Build up the double-twist knot until it is too big to pass back through the hole (left). Starting on the underside of the wing, run the thread up through the wing hole, through the body hole, and down through the other wing hole; then tie a knot (top right). The view of the whiffletree cross bar, seen from the underside, shows how the hanging thread goes down through the bar, across to the other hole, and back up again (bottom right).

and then tie a knot and cut off the twine (FIG. 6-7, top right). Repeat this procedure for the other wing holes. Next, hang the whiffletree from the ceiling—run the cord down from the ceiling, down around and up through the holes on one end of the beam and then back up to the ceiling (FIG. 6-7, bottom right). Repeat the procedure for the other end of the whiffletree, adjust the twine lengths so that it hangs horizontally, and then knot and cut off the twine. When you come to stringing the whiffletree to the wings, run the twine down through one end of the whiffletree, down around, up around, down and up through the wing holes and then back up to the beam. Repeat this procedure with both wings (FIG. 6-8). Finally, tie a length of twine to the underside of the body and add wooden beads until the whole thing is nicely counterbalanced (FIG. 6-8). If all is well, the pteranodon should be balanced so that the slightest air current sets it quietly flapping.

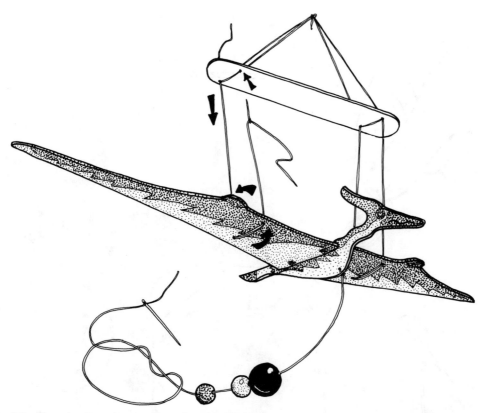

6-8 The wing thread comes down from the hanging bar, twice through the wing holes and then back up to the bar (top). Tie on the counterbalance beads and use a double-twist knot to hold them (bottom).

Hints

- If you decide to go for a much larger toy, still use the $1/8$-inch plywood. If, however, you want to make a much smaller miniature, then consider using $1/16$-inch veneer rather than plywood.
- When you come to thread the wings up to the body, make sure that you leave a gap between the wings and the body so you won't have any problems with wood-to-wood friction and the wings will be free to flap.
- If you use a slow-drying paint, construct a drying line. Since all the components have holes drilled through them, they can be hung from wire hooks.

7

Amy
the Amiable
Ankylosaurus

"BEAUTIFUL AMY, wonderful Amy, beautiful girl of my dreams . . ." And so the song from the 1930s goes, describing in incredibly cloying detail how Amy Johnson the aviator is sugar and spice and all things nice. But the song might well have been written especially for Amy the Amiable Ankylosaurus. We say this, because although the an-ky-low-saw-rus has a reputation for being fearsome, this one is at heart a wonderful, friendly, fluffy sort of character—very much like the girl in the song.

Poor old Amy—everywhere she goes, her dinosaur neighbors take one look at her massive tanklike body—the huge clublike tail, the spike-covered shell, and all the rest—and back off.

Amy sighs . . . it is all the fault of her Canadian plant-eating ankylosaurian ancestors. Apparently, in order to protect themselves from rampaging meat-eating dinosaurs, they had—over many thousands of years—developed and covered their bodies with armor, spines, knobs, spiked balls, horny shells, and a series of heavy macelike tail bones.

Amy looks at her horny, spiked reflection in the pool and groans—is it any wonder that one look is enough to send her dinosaur neighbors running for cover.

Amy flips through *Body Beautiful* magazine. Hmmm . . . perhaps cosmetic surgery is the answer—a little nip and tuck to remove the spikes and tail-clubs, and maybe she would be beautiful. Just like the girl in the song!

Tools and materials

- A sheet of best-quality, white-faced, 1/2-inch-thick multicore plywood, about 12×18 inches, allowing a generous amount for waste and spare
- A 36-inch length of 3/8-inch-diameter dowel, for the axles and the various through-body pivots
- Sixteen 3/4-inch-long round brass-head screws, for fixing the side plates

- Four 3-inch-diameter plastic wheels that are a tight, nonturning fit on the ³/₈-inch-diameter axles
- A quantity of white PVA wood glue
- A small amount of two-tube resin glue
- A sheet of workout paper
- A sheet of tracing paper
- A pencil, ruler, and compass
- A roll each of masking tape and double-sided tape
- An electric scroll saw big enough to cut through a 2-inch thickness of wood
- A press or bench drill with a selection of bits
- A pad or keyhole saw with a fine-toothed blade
- A couple of G-clamps or C-clamps
- A pack of two-tube resin wood filler, light-colored to match the wood
- A pack of graded sandpapers
- Acrylic paints in red, yellow, and black
- A couple of soft-haired paint brushes—one broad and one fine-point
- A can of clear varnish

Looking and planning

Amy the pull-along ankylosaurus is a beautiful moving toy. In use, the wheels turn the axles, the axles turn the cams, and the cams set the body and tail flipping up and down. Great fun! Better still, as the body and the tail move against the chassis, the whole thing makes a really exciting clip-clunking, clitter-clatter noise. It's the perfect toy for active toddlers.

Have a long look at the project picture (FIG. 7-1) and the working drawings (FIG. 7-2), and note how the design is delightfully simple and direct, in that the legs and the axle bearings are cut and worked from the same piece of plywood. Consider how the whole project is layered up from ¹/₂-inch-thick plywood, with the chassis base one thickness, the body three thicknesses, the legs two thicknesses, and so on. Note the way the leg-axle plates are fitted and fixed—two on each side of the chassis—so as to make at one time a pivotal support for the body, the tail, and the axles. The movement is equally ingenious and direct. The egg-shaped cams are set and fixed on the axle, so that as they revolve, they gently tip the body and tail up and down on their shared pivot. It's good fun to watch the cams flip over.

With a project of this type and character, consider how you might possibly modify the techniques to suit your own needs—your skill level, the size of your tool kit, and such. For example, if you enjoy whittling, but are not so happy with the scroll work, then you could whittle a rounded body from solid wood rather than cutting it from plywood. And then again, if you like woodturning, then ditch the ready-made plastic wheels and turn the wheels on the lathe. All such points need to be carefully considered.

Setting out the design, first cuts, and drilling

Study the design templates (FIGS. 7-3 and 7-4). Note that the tail is a single unit that can be traced and cut out separately. See also how the inside legs—back and

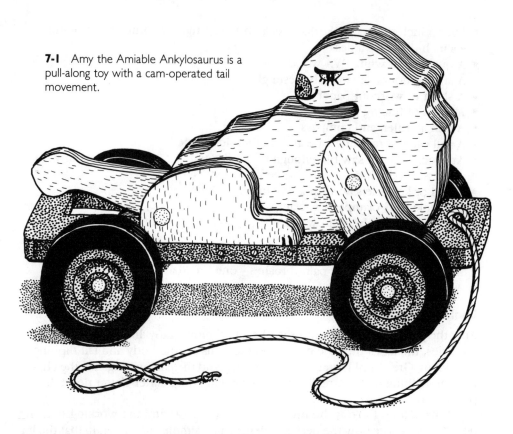

7-1 Amy the Amiable Ankylosaurus is a pull-along toy with a cam-operated tail movement.

front—need to be cut down and modified. When you have a clear understanding of how the toy works, and how it is made and put together, draw the design up to full size and make a tracing. Set the tracing pencil-side down on the plywood and pencil-press transfer the traced lines through to the working face of the wood. Then move to the scroll saw and start by cutting out the single tail profile. Next, swiftly slice the wood down into easy-to-handle shapes. That is to say, quickly saw around the remaining drawn profiles so that the line of cut is about 1/4 inch to the waste side of the drawn line. You can see how the design is made up from a number of repeated components—four back legs, four front legs, four cams, and three bodies. Group and stack the rough-cut profiles according to type. Set strips of double-sided tape between mating surfaces and press them together to make plywood sandwiches (FIG. 7-5, left). If all is well, the body stack will be 1 1/2 inches thick, and the legs stacks each 2 inches thick.

When you are happy with the stacks, use the tracing paper to ensure that the top-of-stack profile is clearly drawn. Having checked and double-checked that all is correct, move the workpiece to the scroll saw, and very carefully cut out the rather complicated profiles. Remember these two main points when you saw: The line of cut should be on the waste side of the drawn line; and the saw blade must run through the wood at right angles to the working face (FIG. 7-5, right). Of course, as you are feeding the wood into the saw, you will need to be variously

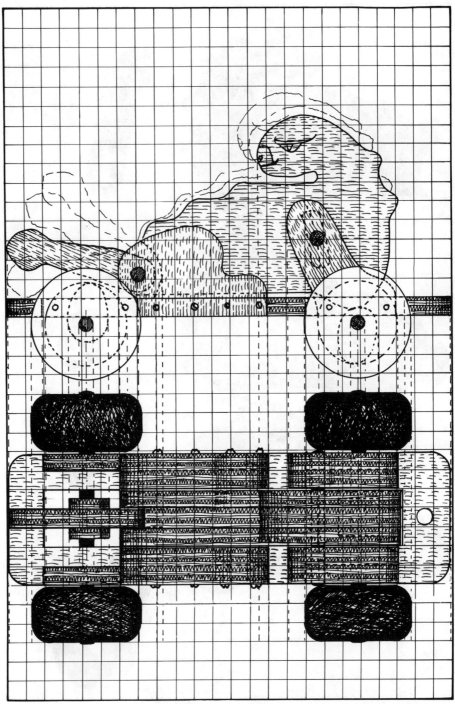

7-2 Working drawing. At a scale of two grid squares to 1 inch, Amy measures 12 inches long, 7 inches high from the ground to the top of the head, and 7 inches wide across the span of the wheels.

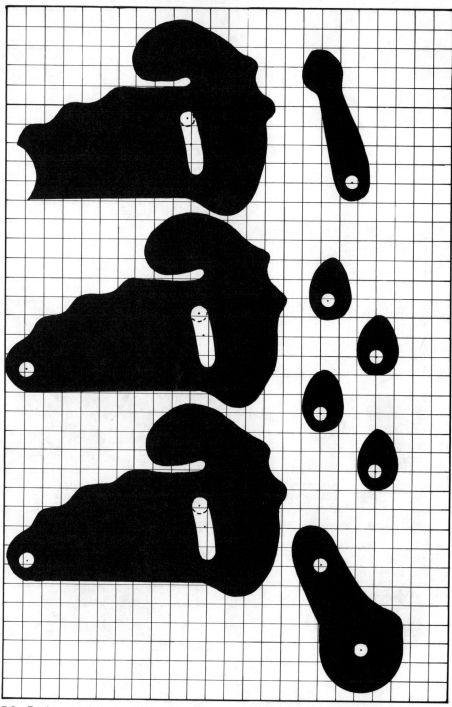

7-3 Design templates for the three body sections, showing the position of the pilot hole and body slot (left), and the tail, cams, and a front leg (right, from top). The scale is two grid squares to 1 inch.

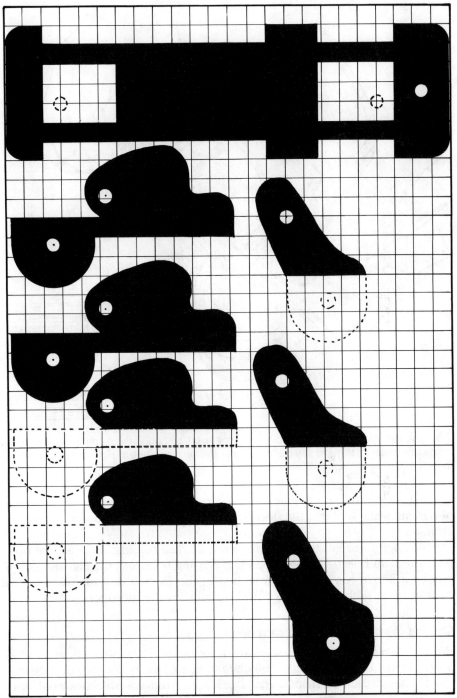

7-4 Design templates for the chassis, showing the position of the pilot holes and the cam holes (top); the four back legs (left); and the three front legs (right). The scale is three grid squares to 1 inch.

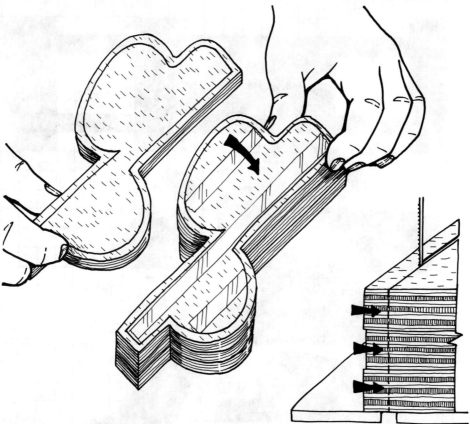

7-5 Use the double-sided tape between mating layers and press the cutouts together to make sandwiched stacks (left). The saw blade must run through the wood at right angles to the working face (right).

holding back, turning, and guiding the wood, to control the speed and direction of the cut. Make sure that the slots on the side of the chassis board are crisp and clean-cut.

When you are finished with the scroll-worked cutouts, establish the precise position of all holes—the pivot holes, the string hole, and the chassis cam pilot holes—and then run them all through with the $3/8$-inch drill bit. Then ease the cams apart and rub them down to a good finish with sandpaper.

Cutting the chassis base and cam holes

Have another good look at the working drawings (FIG. 7-2) and see how the chassis board is made up from a single $1/2$-inch thickness of multicore plywood. Note also how, although each leg-shaped side plate is made from two thicknesses of $1/2$-inch plywood, the inside layer needs to be cut away so that the outside layer becomes a half-lap tenon that can be set in the side of the chassis.

When you have fretted out the 1/2-inch-thick chassis baseboard profile, mark it with a centerline, and then very carefully pencil-press transfer the two cam holes. Bear in mind as you are working that you need to draw certain details with extra care. For example, the cam holes must be carefully aligned on both the centerline and the line of the axles. Spend time getting them just right.

When you come to cutting the cam holes through the chassis board, use the drilled pilot hole as the entry point for the scroll saw blade (FIG. 7-6). Unhitch the blade, pass the blade through the pilot hole, refit and retension the blade, cut out the window of waste, and unhitch the blade to remove the work. You need to repeat the procedure for both cam holes.

Finally, fill any cavities or damage and then use sandpaper to rub down the piece to a smooth-to-the-touch finish. Pay particular attention to edges that are on view.

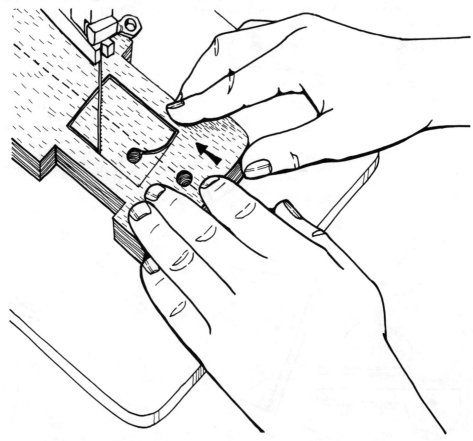

7-6 Use the drilled pilot hole as the entry point for the scroll saw blade and cut out the cam holes or windows in the chassis.

Cutting the leg plates

When you have studied the working drawings and seen how the side plates support both the axles and the through-body pivots, set the eight leg profiles out on the work surface and pencil label them—FRONT LEFT INSIDE, FRONT LEFT OUTSIDE, etc., so that you can see at a glance where they fit. Study the design template (FIG. 7-4), note how the inside plates are reduced, and then draw the new cutting lines on the pieces. Next move the four inside leg plates—two for the back and two for the front—to the scroll saw and cut away the unwanted areas below the chassis-axle pivot (FIG. 7-7). Finally, fill and sand all the cut edges and then regroup the cutouts in pairs and check that all is correct.

Making the body

Once you have cut out the three-thickness body sandwich profile, and drilled and cut the body slot hole, ease the layers apart and remove all traces of tape. Take the middle layer, and use the traced pattern to establish the small tail pivot area that needs to be cut away. See the design template (FIG. 7-3, top left). Do a tryout with

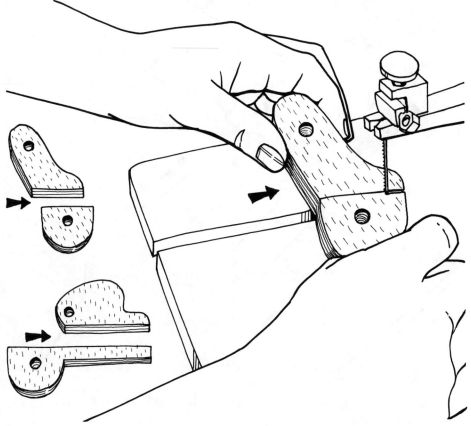

7-7 Cut the unwanted wood away from the inside leg supports.

the tail cutout and a short length of $3/8$-inch-diameter dowel to make sure that the area to be wasted allows for a good degree of swivel movement. When you are happy with the shape and position of the cutting line, move to the scroll saw and cut away the area of waste. Then regroup the three layers with the modified layer at center. Check for fit, fill cavities, and rub down the pieces to a smooth finish.

Painting and putting together

Now you should have completed all the cutouts that make up the toy—the three layers for the body, the chassis base, the four inside leg plates, the four outside leg plates, and the four layers for the two cams. Group them so they are ready for assembly. Bearing in mind that the pieces need plenty of space for easy movement, and allowing for varnish buildup, sand and reduce the thickness of the tail and the inside leg layers by about $1/32$ inch.

Study the painting grid (FIG. 7-8) and note that you will carry out the painting process in two stages. You'll paint the chassis and the bottom of the four outside leg plates red before assembly, but you'll apply the details and the varnish when the toy has been put together.

Wipe away all the dust and mess, move to the area set aside for painting, and set out all your materials. Give the chassis and the bottom of the outside leg plates a couple of coats of red paint, and put them aside to dry.

When the paint is completely dry, establish the length of the axles and through-body pivots, and the position of the cams on the axles. Allow a space of $1/16$ inch between chassis and wheels for easy movement. Glue the three-layer body together and strap the sandwich up with masking tape (FIG. 7-9, top right).

Next, carefully set the outside leg plates in the slots at the edge of the chassis, and screw and glue them into position (FIG. 7-9, bottom left). Check that the axle holes are nicely aligned so that the axles are just clear of the underside of the chassis. Then smear a small amount of glue on the inside faces of the screw-fitted leg plates, and set all the inside leg plates into position. Check the fit, make sure that all the through-leg holes are aligned, and strap them up with masking tape. Pair the cam shapes and glue them together so that you have two 1-inch-wide cams (FIG. 7-9, bottom right).

When the glue is dry, remove all traces of masking tape, set the body between the leg plates, slide the tail in place, make sure that the various holes are aligned, and then run the two through-body dowels into position. If all is correct and as described, the dinosaur should now be sitting on the base, loosely pivoted between the back leg plates.

When you are happy with the fit, take one of the drive axles and slide it through one front leg plate hole, through a cam, and then on through the other leg plate (FIG. 7-10). With the cam set centrally within the cam-drive hole, take the two-tube resin glue and glue-fix both the wheels and the cam in position on the axle. Repeat this procedure at the back, so that all axles, wheels, and cams are fitted and fixed.

Finally, use a fine-point brush to paint in all the little body and feature details, give the whole toy a couple of coats of varnish, tie on the pull-cord, and the toy is finished and ready to go.

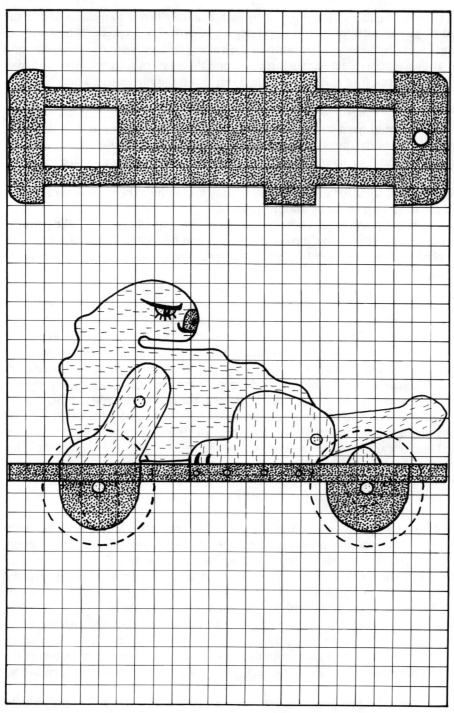

7-8 Painting grid. The scale is two grid squares to 1 inch. *Note:* The wheels have been removed for clarity.

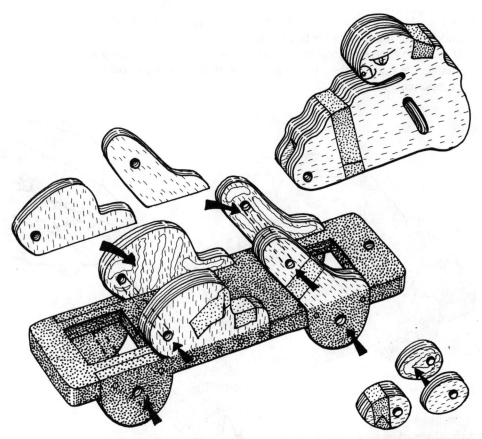

7-9 Glue the three-layer body together and strap the stack up with masking tape (top right). Smear a small amount of glue on the mating faces of the fitted leg plates, and use masking tape to strap the inside leg supports in position (bottom left). Pair the cam shapes and glue and strap them together (bottom right).

Hints

- The relationship between the curve of the cam, the size of the chassis hole, and the shape and fit of the body and tail is crucial. If the cam catches and sticks on the cam hole, or if the through-body dowel is too tight, then be ready to adjust the shape of the cam or the hole, or the size of the through-body pivot holes.
- A good tip when fixing the cams is to tape or wedge the body and tail up out of the way, to allow as much working space as possible.
- If you like the overall project, but want to include woodturning or whittling, then the wheels could be turned, and the dinosaur could be whittled from solid wood.
- If you do decide to make the body from solid wood, make sure—for maximum strength—that the direction of the grain runs from the head down through to the base.

- You could extend the project by making several dinosaurs of different sizes and linking them together like a train.
- If you don't have a scroll saw, you can use a fretsaw or coping saw. Just change the scale of the project to use 1/4-inch-thick plywood and cut out the components in a single thickness.

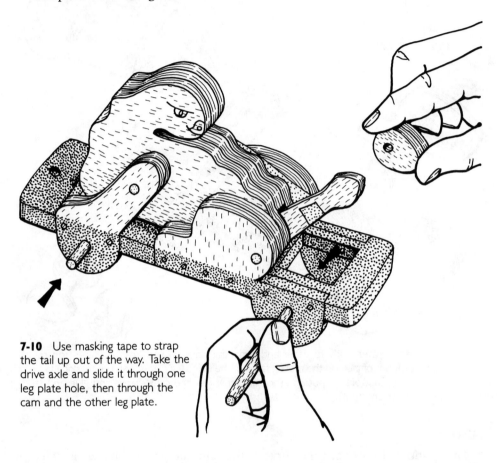

7-10 Use masking tape to strap the tail up out of the way. Take the drive axle and slide it through one leg plate hole, then through the cam and the other leg plate.

8

Rocky the Dancing
Supersaurus Tumbler

POOR OLD ROCKY. As if being bulky, pear-shaped, and wibbly-wobbly wasn't bad enough, he is also a John Doe. The curious fact is, Rocky hasn't been given a proper dinosaur name, because only a few of his ancestors' bones have been found. Be that as it may, when Jim Jenson found the bones—way back in 1972, in a quarry in Colorado—he was amazed by their gigantic size. The shoulder blade alone was over 6 feet, 3 inches in length. Scientists now believe that the supersaurus was one of the largest dinosaurs—perhaps more than 100 feet from nose to tail. Can you imagine how much a supersaurus needed to eat?

Rocky Supersaurus likes nothing better than eating and rock-and-roll dancing. Give him a cookie and put on an Elvis tape, and he's happy. Despite his shape and size, Rocky is an amazingly skillful dancer. Over he goes, does a little dance, and then bobs back up again. Down he goes and up he bobs. Real cool! Down, up, down, up—what fun! What pleasure! Down he goes, and up he comes again.

How does Rocky manage to maintain his get-up-and-go equilibrium? Well . . . that would be telling!

Tools and materials
- A piece of easy-to-turn wood, about 3¼ inches square and 9 inches long (we used beech, but you could use soft maple, cherry, sycamore, or apple)
- A sheet of workout paper
- A sheet of tracing paper
- A pencil and ruler
- A pair of calipers
- A good-sized lathe
- A four-jaw chuck to fit the lathe
- A good selection of wood-turning tools
- A pack of graded sandpapers

- A quantity of lead shot
- A small amount of two-tube resin glue
- A selection of broad and fine-point brushes
- Acrylic paints in green, yellow, and black
- A can of clear, high-shine varnish

Looking and planning

Known in America as Kellys, in England as wibble-wobbles or tumblers, in Germany as *Putzelmann*, in France as *poupee boule*, in Japan as *ot-tok-l*, and in China as *pan-puh-too*, the little tumbler (FIG. 8-1) is one of those traditional, wonderful folk toys that seem to have been with us forever. It's easy to see why children still enjoy playing with tumble dolls—who could not find pleasure in their funny antics and colorful imagery? We think tumblers are fascinating because they just keep bobbing back up—as if by magic!

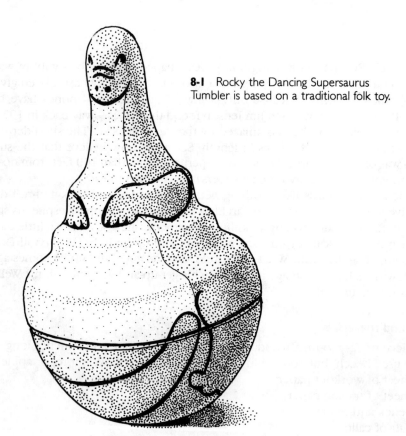

8-1 Rocky the Dancing Supersaurus Tumbler is based on a traditional folk toy.

Have a look at the working drawings and details (FIG. 8-2), and see how, as in most traditional toys, the mechanism is beautifully simple, no more than a low center of gravity and a lead weight concealed in the half-ball base. From the toy-

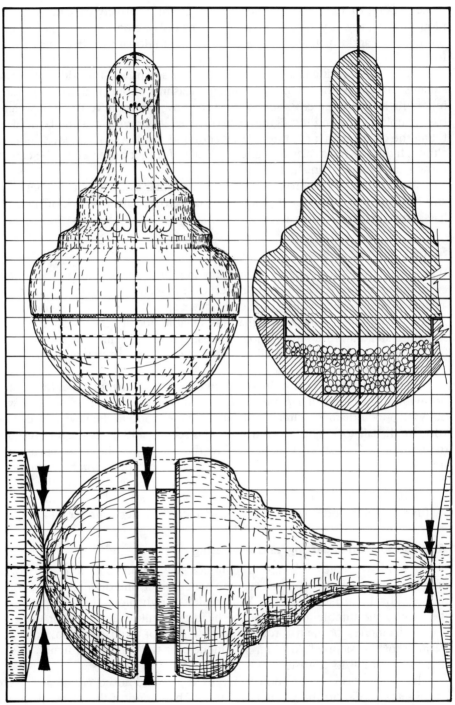

8-2 Working drawing. At a scale of four grid squares to 1 inch, the toy stands about 5 inches high and 3 inches wide. Note the cross section and the lathe details.

maker's point of view, the tumbler is a delightful, relatively easy-to-make, ingenious moving toy. If you have a liking for small playthings, if you enjoy working on the lathe, and if you are looking to make a traditional toy, then this project is for you.

Study the working drawings (FIG. 8-2), and see how, at a grid scale of four squares to 1 inch, this dinosaur tumbler measures about 3 inches wide and 4 inches high. Study the cross section and see how you achieve the lead-weighted base simply by making the figure in two halves, hollowing out the bottom, and filling the cavity with a mixture of lead shot and resin. As to skill level, note that although this toy has a relatively uncomplicated form, it does need to be carefully turned and precisely finished.

Warning: Since this project is primarily a toddler toy, it might well get sucked and chewed, so avoid adding potentially dangerous, easy-to-break-off items like hats, arms, knobs, and the like.

Setting and roughing out

When you have studied the working drawings and details (FIG. 8-2) and have a clear understanding of all the tools, materials, and techniques involved in working a lathe-turned project of this size and character, spend time checking your chosen piece of wood over to make sure that it is suitable. Ideally, the wood needs to be straight-grained and free from knots, warps, splits, and stains. We chose English beech, but you could just as well use lime, cherry, pear, or any number of other easy-to-turn woods.

Establish the end centerpoints by drawing crossed diagonals. Set the compass or dividers to a radius of $1^1/2$ inches and scribe the square-cut ends of the wood out with 3-inch-diameter circles. Then mount the wood in the jaws of the chuck, wind up the tailstock, check that the wood is secure, and bring the tool rest up to the workpiece so that is set slightly below the center of spin. Now, having made sure that you and the lathe are in good safe working order, switch on the power. (See **lathes** and the **lathe safety** checklist in the glossary). Present the chisel to the work, make a few passes to get the feel of the tool and the wood, and then swiftly turn the wood down to a smooth 3-inch-diameter cylinder (FIG. 8-3, top).

Turning the profile, parting, and separating

When you have achieved a smooth cylinder, have another look at the working drawings (FIG. 8-2, bottom). Then take the pencil, ruler, and dividers and set out all the step-offs that make the design. Working left to right along the workpiece, with the base of the tumble toy nearest the headstock, allow 2 inches for the chuck waste, $1^1/4$ inches for the half-round base, $1/4$ inch for the parting tool separation, $1/4$ inch for the stepped lid/plug, $3^1/2$ inches for the top of the figure, and the remainder for tailstock waste (FIG. 8-3, bottom).

Take the tools of your choice—we used a round-nosed gouge and a skew chisel—and round off the shoulders at the lefthand end of the work. Work with the grain, that is, from peak to valley, or from high to low wood, and aim for a flattish half-sphere. When you have achieved what you consider a good half-ball

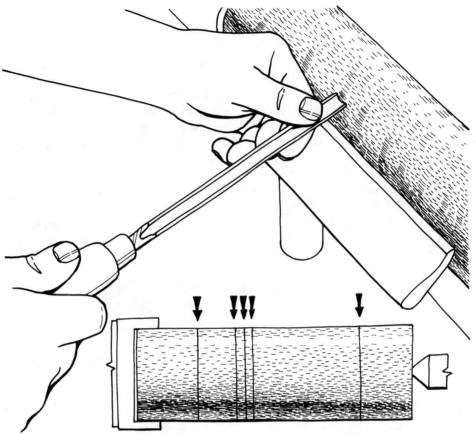

8-3 Use the gouge to rough out the 3-inch-diameter cylinder (top). Mark out the step-offs that make up the design—2 inches for the chuck waste, 1¼ inches for the half-round base, ¼ inch for the parting tool separation, ¼ inch for the stepped lid/plug, and 3½ inches for the top of the figure (bottom).

shape, go to the other end of the workpiece and turn off all the curves and steps that make up the top half of the figure. The work is all easy enough, as long as you try as far as possible to work from the peaks and down into the valleys, and as long as you focus all your attention on the job at hand. Try all the while to search out the finished shape that sits just below the surface of the wood. If necessary, make exploratory drawings and maybe even a Plasticine maquette.

When you have turned the half-ball base and the rippled top-of-figure lid, take a small piece of fine-grade sandpaper and rub the whole workpiece down to a good, smooth finish.

Warning: Wood turning is potentially dangerous, but only if you let your attention wander. Tell companions—friends, family, children, and neighbors—what you are doing so you won't be startled or disturbed. If you are needed in a hurry or an emergency, the best advice is for your friends to switch the power off at the mains, and then to burst into the workshop.

Turning, parting off, and hollow turning

Have another look at the working drawing (FIG. 8-2, bottom), and see how the top half of the turning needs to be parted off in two stages to allow for the stepped lid/plug rim. Take the parting tool and run a 1/2-inch-wide band around the turning—1/4 inch for the parting off, and 1/4 inch for the plug rim—into the wood to a depth of about 3/8 inch. When you are happy with the shape of the plug rim, run the parting tool into the parting-off margin to a depth of about 1 inch. Aim to leave a central core about 1/2 inch in diameter. Now take the skew chisel back to the tail-stock end of the turning, carefully turn the head of the figure down to smooth finish, and part off. Then go back to the central plug rim band, angle the tool, and swiftly turn off the little bevels on the edges of the base and the lid. Now, with the top of the figure carefully cradled and supported in your nonworking hand, run the parting tool straight into the workpiece and part off the top from the base.

With the top of the figure parted off, the half-ball base still held secure in the jaws of the chuck, and the power turned off, move the tailstock well out of the

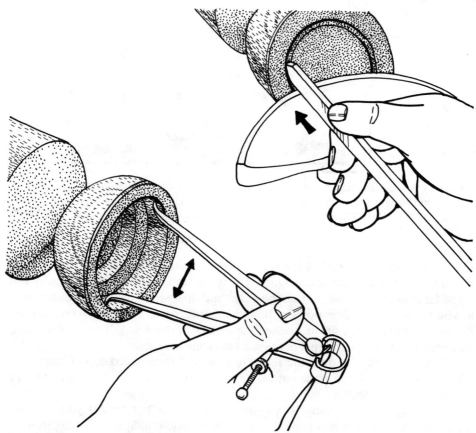

8-4 Run the parting tool into the base to a depth of 1/2 inch to define the edge thickness (top right). Switch off the power to the lathe and use the calipers to check the inside measurement (bottom left).

way, and position the tool rest over the bed of the lathe so that you can work the wood end-on. After using the calipers to measure the diameter of the plug rim on the top half of the figure—it should be about 2 inches in diameter—switch on the power, take the parting tool, and make several sinkings to hollow out the core of the half-ball (FIG. 8-4, top right). Be careful not to run the tool in too deep, and be careful not to knock the workpiece off-center. Go at it nice and easy, and spend time checking your workpiece off against the working drawings. Every now and again along the way, switch off the lathe and use the calipers to check the plug rim-to-base fit (FIG. 8-4, bottom left). Aim for a firm push-fit. Finally, move the tool rest out to the side of the work, support the dishlike turning in your nonworking hand, and use the point of the skew chisel to part the workpiece off from the lathe.

Making the weighted base

Nestle the dishlike base in or on a box or can so that the rim is uppermost and the whole arrangement is stable. Find out how much lead shot you need by filling the bowl to within about 5/8 inch of the rim. Then add the hardener to the resin glue—aim for a thin pourable mix. Next, being careful not to dribble it over the

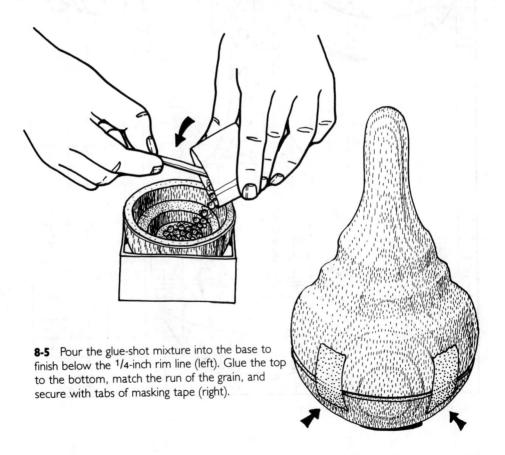

8-5 Pour the glue-shot mixture into the base to finish below the 1/4-inch rim line (left). Glue the top to the bottom, match the run of the grain, and secure with tabs of masking tape (right).

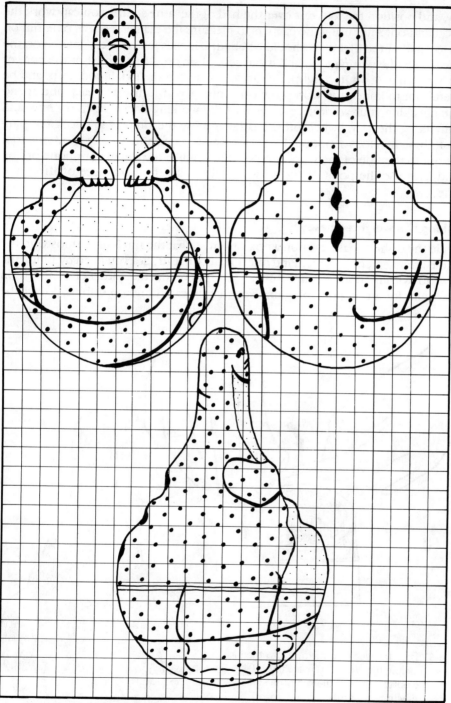

8-6 Painting grid. To achieve the other side view, leave out the tail and reverse the tracing.

rim or over the outside of the turning, pour the resin mixture into the bowl to finish just below 1/4 inch of the rim (FIG. 8-5, left) over the shot. Continue until the bowl is topped up to within 1/4 inch of the rim.

Take the top of the turned figure, smear a little resin over mating faces, very carefully push the rim plug into the base, and carefully align the grain to achieve maximum strength and warp resistance. If all is well, the whole thing should push together for a nice, tight, suction push-fit. Secure with tabs of masking tape (FIG. 8-5, right). Finally, when the resin glue has set, take the graded sandpapers and rub down any dribbles, runs, or smears.

Finishing and painting

Push three long, ball-head pins into the base of the figure—like a three-legged stool—and set it up in your dust-free painting area. Study the working drawings and painting grid (FIG. 8-6); then take a soft pencil and lightly sketch in on the turn-

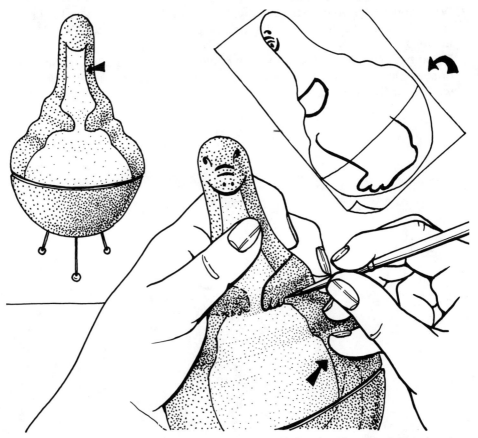

8-7 Paint the body green and the tummy yellow (top left). For the other side view, make a tracing and leave out the tail and add the foot (top right). When you are painting the fine black-line details, support and steady your brush by resting your little finger against the workpiece (bottom).

ing the guide lines that go to make up the main blocks of color—the body and the tummy. Lay on a coat of varnish. When the varnish is completely dry, give the work a light sanding to remove any raised grain hairs, and then paint the body green and the tummy yellow (FIG. 8-7, top left). When the areas of background color are dry, take the pencil and lightly draw in all the black line details (FIG. 8-7, top right). When you are happy with the sketched details, take the fine-point brush and the black paint and paint in all the pencil lines. Steady your brush hand by resting your little finger against the workpiece (FIG. 8-7, bottom). Finally, lay on another couple of coats of varnish and the job is done. Now at last Rocky is ready for his first playroom venture.

Hints

- If you like the idea of making a tumble doll but consider the turning techniques too complicated, you could go for a simple pear shape and settle for having a painted cartoon face.
- When you are turning out the hollow, be careful that you don't make the sides of the half-ball too thin—aim for a base thickness of about 1/8 to 1/4 inch.
- If you can't get hold of lead shot, you could use a piece of salvaged plumbing or solder lead and cast your own plug, or you could pack the cavity with washers or fishing weights.

9

Eddy the Rocking Edmontosaurus

THIS EDMONTOSAURUS (pronounced ed-mont-oh-saw-rus), known to his best boating buddies as Eddy, loves the notion of being a mariner. The sun, the sea, the surf, and a life on the ocean waves—all great! The very idea of being at sea in an open boat, lashed and driven by the wind, is enough to set his blood racing.

Eddy is one of the most handsome of all the dinosaurs. With his huge, flat, duck-billed head; his thousand or so plant-chomping teeth; his wonderful, floppy, loose-skinned, noise-making nose; his webbed feet; and his 42-foot-long body that weighs in at around 3 tons, he cuts quite a dashing figure.

He pulls on his oilskins and his sou'wester and casts off from the quay in his little red rowboat. The pity of it is, that for all his love of the briny, Eddy is prone to seasickness. Once afloat he usually feels nauseously green, bilious, and altogether queasy. But not so this time—he is prepared for the worst! He took his seasickness pills, wore his special acupuncture antiseasickness bracelets, and ate a full breakfast.

Eddy once read somewhere that Admiral Lord Nelson also suffered from seasickness. Eddy's boat rocks up and down, up and down. He'll show them. He was born for the sea—a true sea dog, a son of the sea, an old salt. The blue-green swell lifts his little boat up and down, up and down, up and down. If Nelson could beat the dreaded sickness, then so could he. . . .

Tools and materials
- A sheet of best-quality, white-faced, 3/8-inch-thick multicore plywood, about 12 inches square, allowing for a good amount of placing and cutting waste
- A 3-foot length of 3/8-inch-diameter dowel rod for the pendulum arm
- A 3/4-inch-diameter bead for the pendulum adjustment knob
- A 1 5/8-inch length of thin brass wire for the pendulum pivot
- A selection of 1/2-inch-long brass pins

- A small amount of white PVA wood glue
- A pencil and ruler
- A sheet of workout paper
- A sheet of tracing paper
- A coping saw
- A bench hook
- Two small clamps
- A try square
- A workbench with a vise
- A drill with bits $3/8$ inch, $1/4$ inch, and $3/32$ inch in diameter
- A small hammer and a punch
- A small amount of two-tube resin filler
- A pack of graded sandpapers
- Acrylic paints in red, green, yellow, white, light blue, dark blue, and black
- A couple of soft-haired paintbrushes—one broad and one fine-point
- A tin of clear, high-shine varnish

Looking and planning

The edmontosaurus pendulum is a classic rock-the-child-to-sleep toy (FIG. 9-1). This toy is usually fixed high up on a wall, like a clock. An adult sets the pendulum swinging, and the resulting motion of Eddy rocking back and forth in his rowboat lulls the child to sleep. Of course, when the tot becomes a toddler, he or she will be able to adjust the position of the pendulum bob, and in so doing, observe the curious fact that the longer the distance between the pivot and the pendulum bob, the slower the rate of swing. It's a good, fun, educational toy.

Have a look at the working drawing (FIG. 9-2), and see how, at a scale of four grid squares to 1 inch, the main body of the toy measures 6 inches wide, $5^1/2$ inches high, and $1^3/4$ inches deep from front to back. Note the use throughout of laminated $3/8$-inch multicore plywood, with the main body being made up of five thicknesses, and the boat and the pendulum fish each being made up of two thicknesses. Study the cross section (FIG. 9-3, top right), and see the way the two-thickness boat-dinosaur is contained and pivoted within a three-thickness cavity. Note the washers at front and back of the boat.

The six L-shaped spacers—three on either side—are shaped and fitted in such a way that they distance the front plate from the back plate, while at the same time acting as a stop point that marks the maximum swing of the pendulum rod.

The fish-shaped pendulum bob is made of two thickness of plywood sandwiched together, with the position of the bob on the pendulum rod fixed by a bead-topped wedge-peg. The pendulum rod slides through a loose-fit hole or passage that runs top to bottom through the fish. The peg hole is placed so that the wedge jams the pendulum rod tight against the side of its passage. We have allowed for a pendulum dowel of about 36 inches long. Note that, because of page length, the illustrations only show a short section of pendulum rod.

Eddy the Rocking Edmontosaurus is a simple, easy-to-make toy that can be put together with a few inexpensive tools and a minimum of expertise.

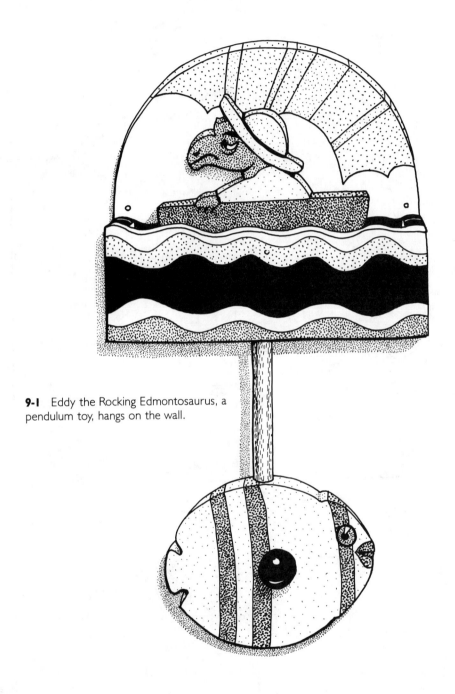

9-1 Eddy the Rocking Edmontosaurus, a pendulum toy, hangs on the wall.

Setting out the design and using the coping saw

When you have studied the design templates (FIG. 9-4), draw the design up to full size and make a clear tracing. Check that the plywood is sound and free from flaws. When you have decided how to space the profiles so as to leave as little

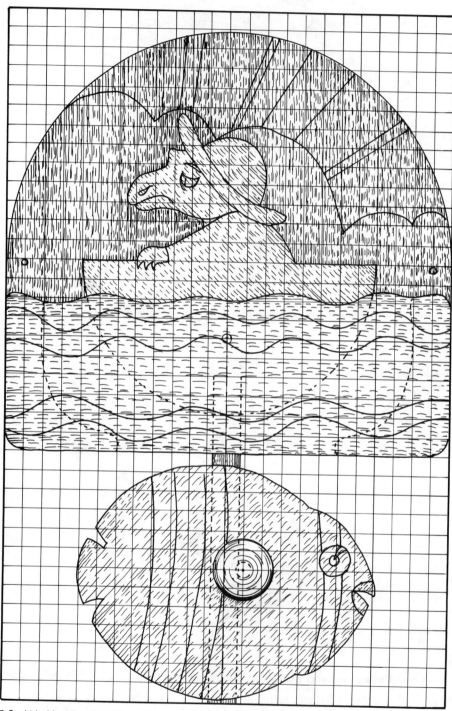

9-2 Working drawing. The scale is four grid squares to 1 inch. Note that the pendulum arm is not shown to length.

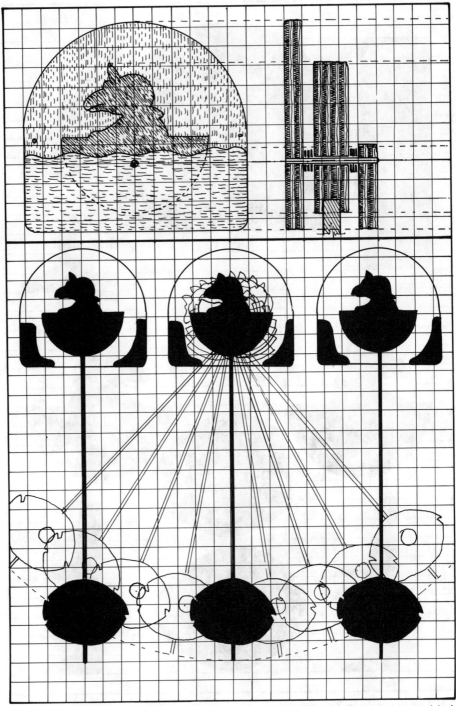

9-3 Working drawing. For the front and cross section, the scale is two grid squares to 1 inch (top). The bottom portion, showing the toy in use, is not drawn to scale.

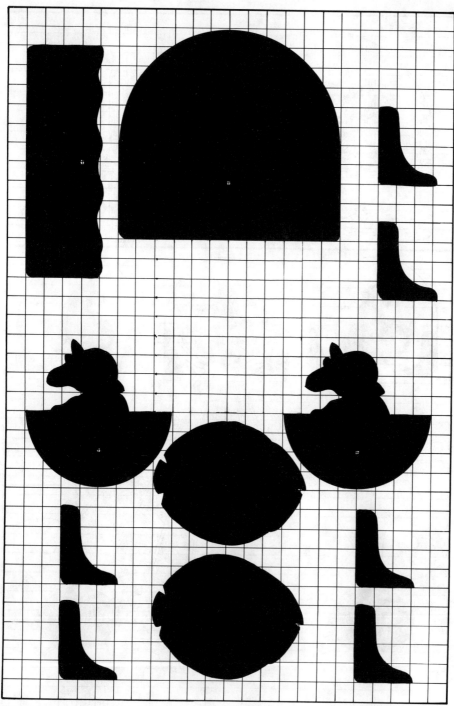

9-4 Design templates. The scale is two grid squares to 1 inch.

waste as possible, fix the tracing in place with a few tabs of masking tape and carefully pencil-press transfer the traced lines through to the wood. When you are done, hinge the tracing back out of the way, make any necessary adjustments to the forms or to the density of the lines, and then label all the drawn profiles. You should have 12 plywood components in all—one large, arched back board, six L-shaped spacers, a single "wave" front board, two rowboat-dinosaurs, and two fish pendulum bobs.

When you are happy with the transferred images, peel off the tracing paper and take the plywood to the vise and workbench. Set the tension of the coping saw blade in its frame and make sure that you have a supply of spare blades. Start by cutting the plywood down into small, easy-to-handle pieces. To do so, swiftly run the line of cut about a ¼ inch to the waste side of the drawn line. Be watchful that the rate of cut is not so slow, nor so forceful, that the saw blade tears up the grain and damages the drawn line.

When you have achieved all 12 rough-sawn cutouts, secure them a piece at a time in the vise, and set to work carefully fretting out the profiles (FIG. 9-5, left).

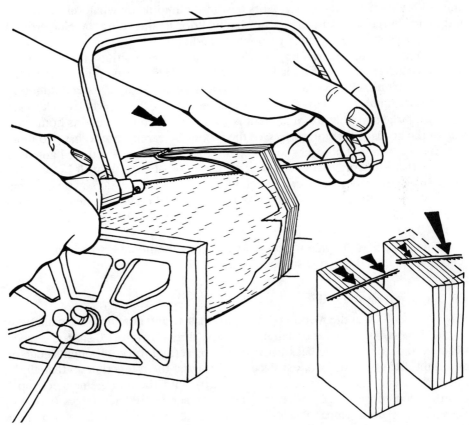

9-5 Secure the rough-sawn shape in the vise and carefully fret out the profile (left). If you twist the blade, the cut will be distorted (bottom right).

The work is all pretty straightforward, as long as you run the line of cut just fractionally to waste side of the drawn line, hold the saw so that the blade is running through the wood at right angles to the working face, and adjust the wood in the vise so that the blade is always presented with the most efficient line of next cut. Keep the saw moving at a steady even pace, all the while being careful not to force or twist the blade. *Note:* If the blade is twisted or bent, the cut will be distorted (FIG. 9-5, bottom right).

Laminating, gluing, pinning, and punching

With all 12 plywood components nicely fretted out, have a fresh look at the working drawings (FIGS. 9-2 and 9-3), and see how variously the cutouts needs to be layered and laminated.

Arrange and stack the cutouts, and label them clearly to establish which of the faces is to be hidden and which is to be on view. For example, with the six L-shaped spacers, stack them up so that you have two well-matched groups of three, and label the stacks LEFT and RIGHT. If you feel that one or other of the cutouts within such and such a stack fits best in the middle or whatever, then label and pencil in registration marks accordingly. Prior to spreading the glue around, you need to know clearly what goes where and how.

When you have layered up and labeled the various cutouts, clear the work surface of all debris, and be ready with the glue, panel pins, punch, and small hammer. Starting with, say, the two fish cutouts that make up the pendulum bob, smear a small amount of PVA glue on mating faces, bring the two sticky faces together, make sure that the alignment is good, and then tap the pins home, and punch the heads below the surface of the wood. Be careful not to have so much glue that it oozes out all over the place, and make sure when you are banging in the pins that the layers stay put and don't slide out of alignment. It helps if you push the edges hard up against a bench hook (FIG. 9-6, left). And so you continue with all the other laminations that make up the toy. When you come to doing the three-layer L-shaped pieces, the gluing and pinning has to be done in two stages (FIG. 9-6, right).

Finally—when the glue is dry—take the graded sandpapers and rub the layered components down to a smooth-edged finish.

Putting together and drilling

Have another look at the working drawings (FIG. 9-3), and note how the main body of the toy is made by sandwiching the two three-thickness L-shaped spacers between the front and the back boards. Start by setting the components edge-on and right-side-up on the work surface and bringing them together so that all the edges are nicely aligned. When you are happy with the arrangement, clamp it together and run a couple of registration lines across the side edges (FIG. 9-7). Remove the clamps, smear a small amount of glue on mating surfaces, bring the parts together and fix with pins. Again, make sure that when you are banging in the pins the glued layers don't slide out of alignment. Pressing the sides up against the bench hook will help keep everything aligned.

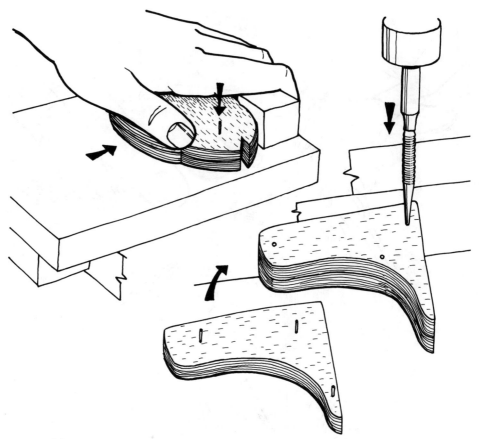

9-6 When you pin the layers together, push the edges hard up against the bench hook so that they are aligned (left). Glue and pin the L shapes in two stages: First punch the pin heads below the surface, and then glue and pin the third lamination in place (right).

The design of this toy is such that the holes all need to be precisely placed and worked. For example, with the fish bob, while one hole has to run top to bottom through the layered material, a secondary hole has to run from face to face through the thickness of the ply so that it intersects and is at right angles to the first hole. The hole that runs through the main body of the toy and the rowboat has to be set so that when the boat pivots, it moves squarely to the front and back faces of the body cavity.

Starting with the main pivot hole that runs through the body, first fix the precise position of the hole, and then pack the cavity with bits of scrap plywood and support the workpiece on scrap wood. Then take the drill and the 3/32-inch bit and run the hole from front to back, through the wave board, through the scrap, and through the back board (FIG. 9-8, top).

Once you have established the position of the holes, secure the fish bob in the vise so that the top edge is uppermost. Take the drill and the 3/8-inch bit and

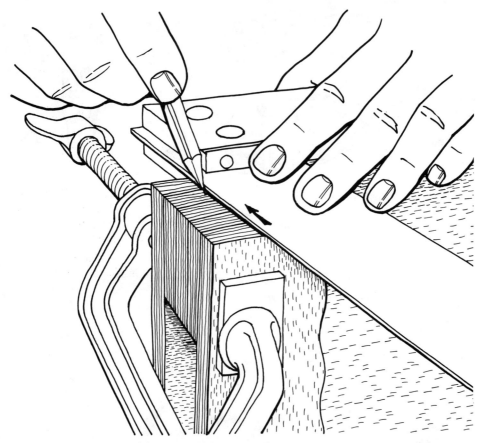

9-7 When the component edges are nicely aligned, clamp them in place and use the try square and pencil to mark registration lines on the side edges.

sink a hole down through the height of the fish bob. Be sure to hold and align the drill so that the hole runs squarely through the $^3/_4$-inch thickness of the plywood. Run the drill through the hole several times to ensure a loose fit for the $^3/_8$-inch dowel (FIG. 9-8, bottom).

Set the fish flat-face-down on a piece of scrap wood, and slide a length of waste $^3/_8$-inch dowel through the shaft hole. Next, after you have fixed the position of the wedge-peg hole, take the drill and the $^1/_4$-inch bit, and sink the hole through the bob thickness. If all is well, the drill bit should run through the wood so that it takes a very small, glancing cut or bite out of the side of the scrap dowel.

Secure the rowboat bottom-side-up in the vise and use the $^3/_8$-inch bit to sink the pendulum shaft hole in to a depth of about $^3/_4$ inch. Then use the $^3/_{32}$-inch bit to run the pivot hole through the thickness of the rowboat (FIG. 9-9, top).

Finally, cradle the wedge-peg bead in a hole drilled in a piece of scrap wood, and sink a $^1/_4$-inch-diameter hole into your chosen bead to a depth of about $^1/_4$ inch (FIG. 9-9, bottom left).

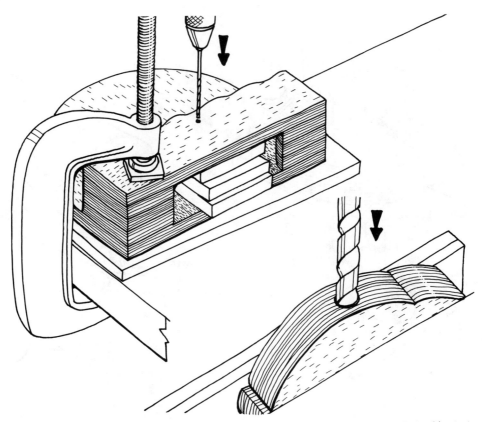

9-8 Pack the cavity with scrap plywood, hold the work with a clamp, and drill the 3/32-inch-diameter hole in from front to back (top). When you drill the hole in the pendulum bob, run the drill through several times to ensure a loose fit for the 3/8-inch-diameter dowel (bottom).

Fitting the wedge-peg and dowel shaft

When you have created the various holes, you can begin the pleasurable task of putting the toy together. Start by gluing and fitting a little scrap of dowel in the bead hole. When the glue is dry, whittle the dowel to a sharp pencil-point finish (FIG. 9-9, right). If all is correct, you should be able to push the peg home so that the bead knob is flush with the face of the fish and so that the fish is a firm wedge-fix on the dowel shaft. For a good, firm fit, you might well need to adjust the hole or the shape of the wedge-peg.

Score the end of the pendulum dowel, smear it with glue, push it in the hole in the bottom of the boat, and put the assembly to one side to dry. When the glue is dry, have a tryout by pivoting the rowboat in position.

Painting and finishing

When you are happy with the overall fit and action of the toy, take the graded sandpapers and rub all the faces, edges, and corners down to a smooth finish. Pay

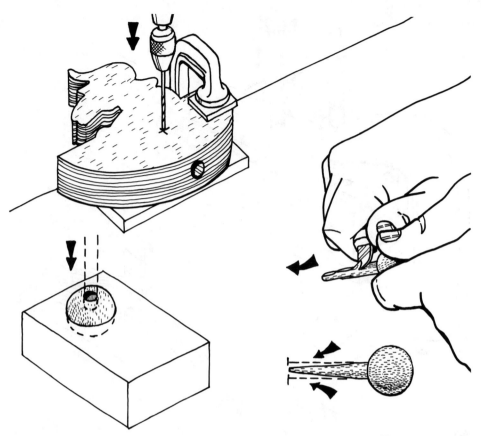

9-9 Run the pivot hole through the thickness of the rowboat (top). Cradle the wedge-peg bead in a hole drilled in some scrap wood, and sink a $1/4$-inch-diameter hole into the bead to a depth of about $1/4$ inch (bottom left). Whittle the dowel to a point (right).

special attention to the details of the dinosaur, the top of the waves, and the fish profile.

Make a tracing of all the design details (FIG. 9-10), and pencil-press transfer the traced lines through to the various faces of the toy. Then wipe off all the dust and move to the area that you have set aside for painting. Cover the work surface with newspaper, set out your chosen colors, and generally make ready. Fit each of the pieces to be painted with little thumb-pin legs, so that once painted they can be set down without the wet paint coming into contact with the work surface.

The painting of this particular project is slightly unusual, in that it has so many areas of color. In this case, rather than laying on large areas of ground color and then painting on secondary colors, you will find the process much easier if you block in the various areas and paint up to a drawn line. The general procedures are the same; the only real difference is that when you come to blocking in neighboring colors, you must make sure that the first color is dry before you lap over with the next color, to achieve a clean painted edge.

9-10 Painting grid. Paint the interior areas, the side, and the bottom of the sea dark blue.

Paint the main body of the fish, the dinosaur's oilskins, and the sun rays yellow; the boat and the lips and stripes on the fish bright red; the clouds and two of the wave-stripes white; the sky and one of the waves stripes light blue; the bottom wave, the eye of the fish, and the dinosaur face green; the various small details black and white, and so on.

Note: The side spacers and the whole interior need to be painted dark blue. As they are so difficult to get at, you should paint them first. When the paint is completely dry, lay on several coats of varnish and put to one side to dry.

When the varnish is dry, assemble the toy, and put the boat in position. Cut the brass pivot pin to size, set the brass washers between the layers, and slide the pivot pin in place through the front board, the washers, the rowboat, the next washers, and on through the back board (FIG. 9-11). Fix the brass pin at the front and back with a small glued-wedge splinter, make good with filler, rub down, paint, and varnish. Finally, hang the toy on the wall, glide the fish onto the pendulum dowel, adjust the wedge-peg bead, and Eddy is ready!

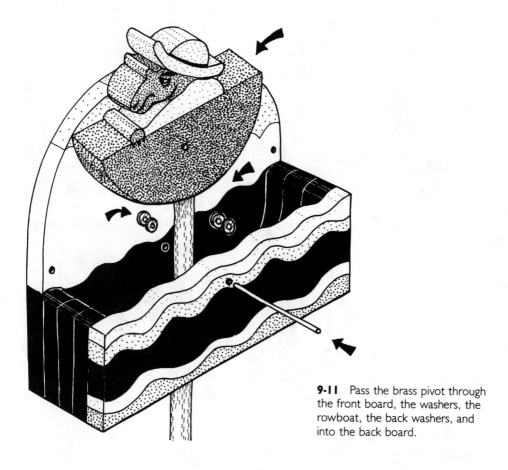

9-11 Pass the brass pivot through the front board, the washers, the rowboat, the back washers, and into the back board.

Hints

- Chances are you will have to use a small amount of filler to make good nicks or damage. We prefer to use two-tube resin filler because it sets to a good finish and stays put. Plaster filler, on the other hand, has a tendency to crack and fall out.
- In the context of using a coping, piercing, or fretsaw to cut thin sheet wood, the rate of cut means the up-and-down speed of the blade in relationship to the amount of pressure put on the saw and the time taken to saw through a given thickness and length of wood. Go for a fast up-and-down blade speed and a small amount of push-forward pressure. Certainly, this way of working results in a slow-moving line of cut, but then again, the cut line is clean, smooth-edged, and at a good angle to the working face.
- The thinner the pivot rod, the less friction and, consequentially, the better the movement of the object being pivoted. For a super-smooth movement, you could line the through-boat pivot hole with a metal tube or bush.
- When you come to hanging the toy on the wall, use two fixings—one on each side—so it will stay put when the pendulum is swung into motion.

10
Sam-Sung the Skedaddling Scelidosaurus

THIS DELIGHTFUL SCELIDOSAURUS—pronounced skel-ide-oh-saw-rus, meaning "limb lizard"—is known by her close friends as Sam. With her small, delicate head; charming, leaflike, ridged teeth; four shapely legs; and body most attractively bejeweled with bony knobs, she is a noted Tibetan beauty. And, as if being delicate, charming, and beautiful isn't enough, Sam-Sung is a highly skilled Sherpa. That is to say, Sam is one of a Tibetan people living on the southern slopes of the Himalayas in Nepal who are famous as mountaineers.

Now, Sam-Sung is not what you might call an orthodox climber. She doesn't much care for all the usual climbing gear and paraphernalia—the ropes, rings, pegs, sliding tackle, crampons, and all the rest—she just bounces to the top of the slopes, and then, just as swiftly, skips and skedaddles back down again. Certainly her downslope action is not exactly poetry in motion—she has been likened to a shuffling, shambling, skip-hopping kangaroo—but, goodness, it's an efficient way of traveling down a slope!

Tools and materials
- A piece of best-quality, easy-to-carve, 5/8-inch-thick wood, about 8×4 inches, for the body (we used linden, or lime, wood)
- A sheet each of 1/4- and 3/4-inch-thick, best-quality multicore plywood, 4×4 inches, for the arms and legs
- A couple of pieces of dowel—a 2-inch length at 1/4-inch diameter, and a 4-inch length at 1/8-inch diameter
- A C-clamp (also called a G-clamp)
- A small amount of white PVA glue
- A small amount of double-sided tape
- A small amount of Super Glue fast-drying adhesive
- A pencil and ruler

- A sheet of tracing paper
- A sheet of workout paper
- A coping saw
- A small hand drill with $1/4$- and $1/8$-inch-diameter bits
- A small knife for whittling—we use a penknife
- A small U-section spoon or scoop gouge
- A pack of graded sandpapers
- Acrylic paints in yellow, green, red, white, and black
- A small amount of clear, high-shine varnish
- Two $1/4$-inch brass washers

Looking and planning

The skedaddling scelidosaurus (FIG. 10-1) is one of those delightful, traditional, simple movement toys—like yo-yos, swinging gymnasts, balancing birds, and one or two others—that have been with us for so long that we tend to take them for granted and never bother to figure out how they do what they do. Certainly, kids never cease asking questions, but we've got a feeling that adults never get around to answering. And so it is with the skedaddling scelidosaurus. Kids love to start her off at the top of an inclined board and watch her as she waddles and trundles unaided down the slope. They invariably ask how it works, but up until now we've never gotten around to thinking it out. Well . . . just in case you are asked the dreaded question—here goes. It's all done by weight and counterbalance. As the feet rock, the seesaw action of the pivoted body shifts the weight, which in turn provides forward momentum, which in turn results in the feet rocking, which in turn results in the seesaw body shifting on its pivot, which in turn pro-

10-1 Sam-Sung the Skedaddling Scelidosaurus, a simple movement toy, skips and trundles down an inclined plane.

vides forward momentum . . . and so on, ad infinitum. No doubt if the slope was long enough, and not too slippery nor too rough, and if someone was around to give the occasional helping prod, the toy would skip, waddle, and hop on and on, forever. Well, there you go—we're still not so sure that's much of an answer, but at least we tried.

Have a look at working drawings (FIG. 10-2) and see how, at a scale of four grid squares to 1 inch, the toy stands about 3 inches high, about 7 inches long from nose to tail, and about 2^1/$_2$ to 3 inches wide across the span of the legs. Note the two-thickness construction of the legs, and the seesaw movement of the body on the through-body leg-to-leg pivot. Study the plan view and consider the way the 5/8-inch thickness of the wood is divided and whittled up and down the length of the back so that each of the peaks finishes up as two side-by-side pointed knobs. The construction is such that the 1^1/$_8$-inch width across the span of the front arms allows the front of the toy to swing and dip freely between the feet. The legs are built out at the hips so that the feet are 1^1/$_4$ inches apart. The body is lightly worked with the spoon gouge to give the toy a scaly texture.

Finally, consider how the angle of the inclined board down which the toy trundles depends on the balance and weight of the toy and the texture and friction between the plank and the feet. We tried out various surfaces, everything from a high-shine plastic varnish to carpet-covered plank. At the end of it all, we came to the conclusion that planed, unpolished wood makes the best surface.

Setting out and fretting out

When you have clear understanding of just how the project needs to be worked— the tools, the materials, and the order of work—set the wood out on the work surface and check it over for quality. The plywood should be free of warps, splits, and delaminations. The quality of the easy-to-carve wood is more of a problem. After you check that the grain is smooth and free from knots and splits, take a small, sharp knife and have a trial cut. The blade needs to slip through the grain with a minimum of force to leave the cut face looking smooth and shiny. If the wood cuts ragged, or blunts the tool, try another variety. We used lime wood, sometimes called linden, but you can choose from many other types. If in doubt, ask your supplier for advice and see if he or she will let you have a tryout on scraps of various white woods.

When you are happy with your chosen materials, study the design templates (FIG. 10-3), trace off the forms that make up the design—the body, legs, arms, and hip pieces—and pencil-press transfer the traced images through to the appropriate wood. The body needs to be on the 5/8-inch-thick, easy-to-carve wood, the arms and the hip pieces on the 1/4-inch-thick plywood, and the legs on the 3/4-inch plywood. Make sure that the lines and the hole centers are well established, and pay particular attention to the registration marks on the hip spacers and leg pieces (FIG. 10-4, top).

Take the wood a piece at a time, secure it in the jaws of the vise, and then set to work with the coping saw. With the blade well-tensioned in the frame of the saw and the saw blade running through the wood at a right angle to the working

Bones the Confused Dinosaur

Dinosaur Puzzle

Dashing Dinosaur Driver

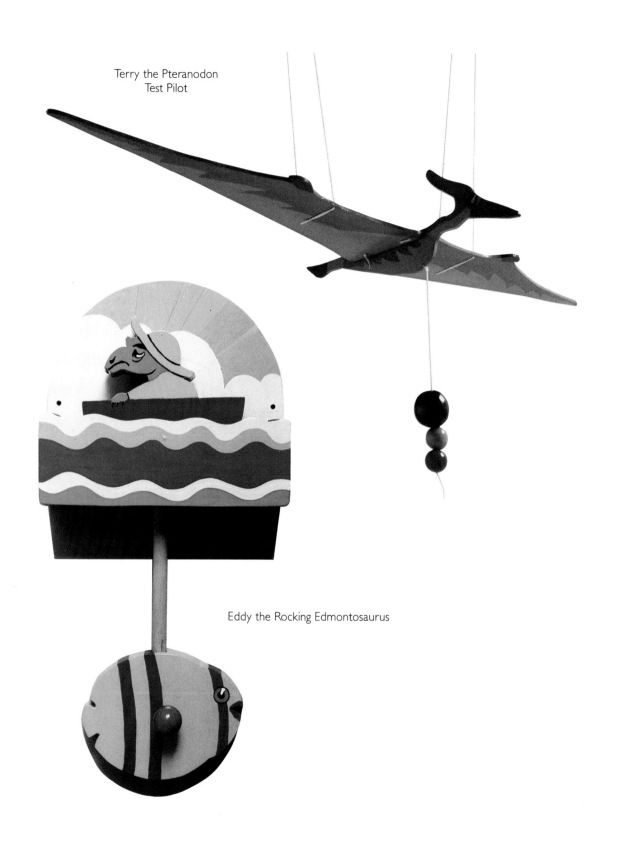

Terry the Pteranodon
Test Pilot

Eddy the Rocking Edmontosaurus

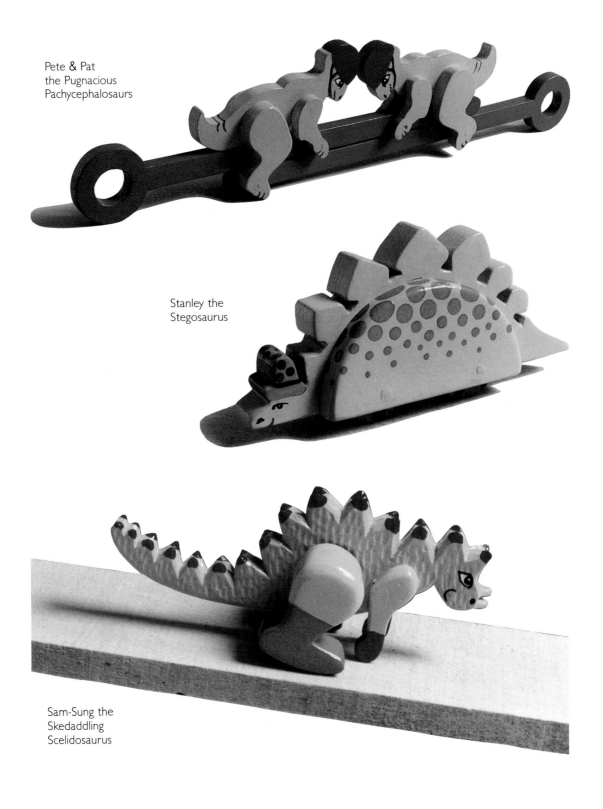

Pete & Pat
the Pugnacious
Pachycephalosaurs

Stanley the
Stegosaurus

Sam-Sung the
Skedaddling
Scelidosaurus

Mavis the
Maiasaura Mom

Dinosaur Movie Stars

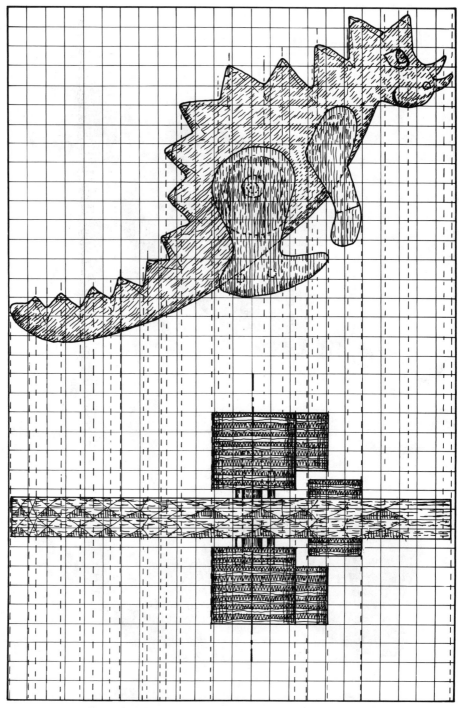

10-2 Working drawing. At a scale of four grid squares to 1 inch, Sam-Sung measures about 7 inches from nose to tail, 3 inches wide, and 4 to 5 inches high.

10-3 Design template. The scale is four grid squares to 1 inch. Note the registration points at the top of the legs and hips.

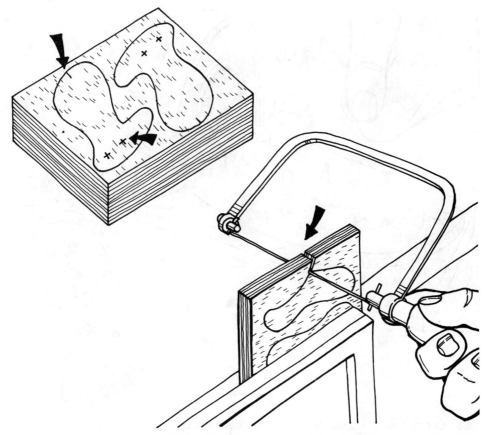

10-4 Make sure that the traced lines, the hole centers, and the registration points are clearly marked and set out (top). Run the line of cut slightly to the waste side of the drawn line (bottom).

face, carefully fret out the profiles. Work at a steady, easy pace, all the while keeping the wood moving so that the saw is always presented with the line of best cut. Also make sure that the line of cut runs slightly to the waste side of the drawn line (FIG. 10-4, bottom).

Note: When you are cutting out the body, be extra careful not to twist the blade and so split the grain.

Drilling and laminating

Have a good look at the working drawings and details and see how you need to drill seven holes in all—a single $1/4$-inch hole through the body, a $1/4$-inch hole through each of the two hip discs, and two $1/8$-inch holes halfway through the thickness of each of the two feet. First fix the precise position of all seven holes. Then take the drill and the appropriate bit, hold the work secure, and work the holes accordingly. Run the bit several times through the body hole so that the $1/4$-inch-diameter dowel is a loose and easy fit (FIG. 10-5, top).

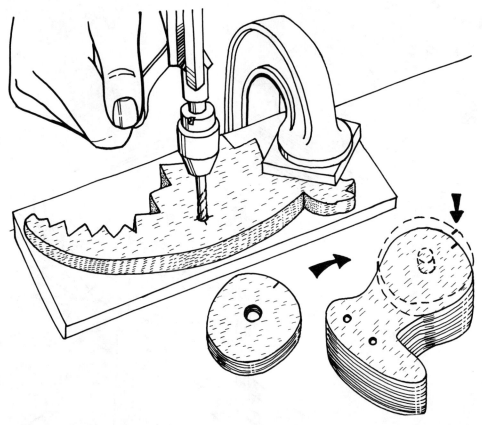

10-5 Drill the hole so that the ¹/4-inch-diameter dowel is a loose fit through the body hole (top). When you come to gluing the hip piece to the top of the leg, check that the registration marks are carefully aligned (bottom).

With all the holes drilled, take the two hip discs, and, one piece at a time, glue-fix them in place on the inside faces of the two legs. Make sure that the hip holes and the top-edge profile are perfectly aligned by matching up the registration points (FIG. 10-5, bottom).

Whittling, shaping, and gouging

Study the working drawing again (FIG. 10-2). Then take the body piece in one hand and the small sharp knife in the other, and start swiftly removing all the sharp edges. Work with a tight, thumb-controlled paring action—just as you might pare the skin from an apple—and run the chamfer around all edges of the body. Under the chin, down and around the belly, up and over each of the spine knobs and so on. Carve a chamfer on both sides of the body. Little by little, open up each of the between-knob valleys by running the chamfer out over the side faces of the wood (FIG. 10-6, top).

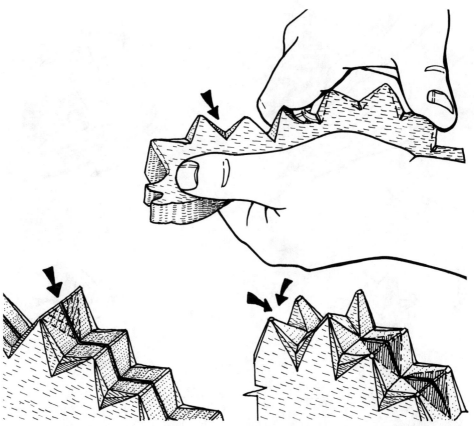

10-6 Open up each of the between-knob valleys by running the chamfer out and over the side face of the wood (top). Cut in the line of the spine with a continuous V-section groove (bottom left). Gradually widen and deepen the central groove until each of the spine knobs is a separate pyramid shape (bottom right).

When you have whittled and rounded each of the knobs, run the point of the knife down the center of the back to cut through and divide each of the peaks, and establish the spine with a continuous cut-in V-groove (FIG. 10-6, bottom left). Run the groove from the end of the tail through the top of the head. Next, widen and deepen the central V-groove until each peak or knob has been split down the center and is as deep as the between-point valleys (FIG. 10-6, bottom right). When each spine knob has been worked so that it is a separate pyramid, go over the workpiece to bring it to a good finish.

When you have achieved a nicely carved body shape, take the small U-section gouge and swiftly cut in all the little dapples to make the rippled texture of the scales. Don't fuss around too much. Simply start at the head and work down towards the tail, all the while working across the grain and removing little scooping curls of waste (FIG. 10-7, top left). Whittle the two nose peaks to blunt points (FIG. 10-7, bottom), and, finally, give the whole workpiece a rubdown with fine sandpaper (FIG. 10-7, top right).

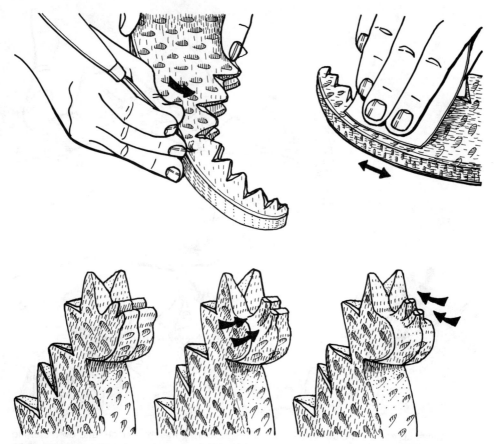

10-7 Working across the grain, make the rippled texture of the scales by removing little scooped curls of waste (top left). Whittle the nose peaks to a blunt point by making scooping cuts from side to center (bottom). Working with the grain, use a fine-grade sandpaper to rub the surface down to smooth finish (top right).

Putting together

Have a fresh look at the working drawings (FIG. 10-2), and see how the total body-and-arms piece nicely seesaws on the through-body pivot, with the head end slightly heavier than the tail. Have a dry-run fitting to make sure the toy will operate properly. Slide the main pivot dowel through the body hole, pop the washers onto the dowel, slide the hip-leg pieces over the ends of the dowels, and set the two short lengths of 1/8-inch-diameter dowels into place in the foot holes (FIG. 10-8, top). At this stage, the body should be balanced so that the tail is slightly dipped down. Next tack the arms in place to the front of the body with tabs of double-sided tape, and try various arm angles until you achieve a good seesaw balance. Aim for a balance with the nose of the dinosaur dipping down so that it is more or less at the same level as the end of the tail; the front paws should rest on the ground. When you have got it right, use a pencil to draw

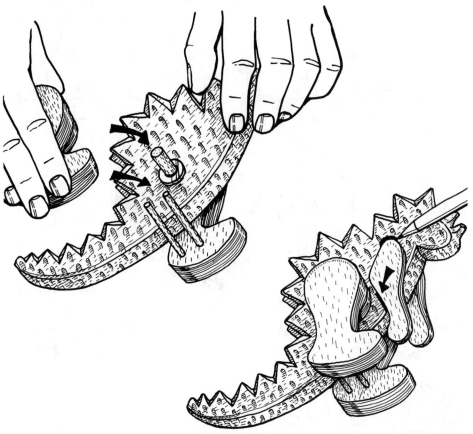

10-8 Slide the main pivot dowel through the body, slip the washers and leg-hip pieces on, and push the two $1/8$-inch-diameter foot-stop dowels into place in the foot holes (top). Use a pencil to draw registration marks around the arms (bottom).

around the arms (FIG. 10-8, bottom), make a couple of registration marks, and then glue-fix the arms on either side of the body. Finally, adjust all the dowel lengths for a perfect fit, glue the dowel ends, and put the toy back together.

Painting and finishing

When you are happy with the toy, wipe off all the dust and move to the area that you have set aside for painting. Cover the work surface with newspaper and set out the paints and brushes so they are comfortably at hand. You won't need a drying rack or line, because the toy is so tricky to paint and acrylics are so fast-drying that you will always be able to find a dry area to hold.

After you have studied the painting grid (FIG. 10-9), start by painting the whole toy yellow. When the yellow ground coat is dry, see if you need to lay on a second coat. If you do, give the toy a swift rubdown with a fine-grade sandpaper before you apply the second coat. Next, paint the boots green, the gloves and the back

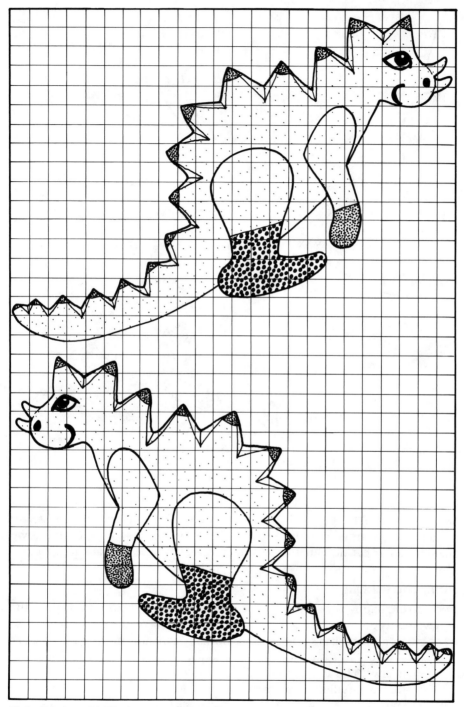

10-9 Painting grid. The body is yellow, the boots bright green, the gloves and knobs bright red, and the eye details black and white.

knobs red, the eyes white, and the two $1/8$-inch dowels and the details of the face black. When the acrylics are completely dry, give the whole toy a couple of coats of varnish and put it aside to dry. Finally, give Sam-Sung a test waddle on a length of smooth, unpolished plank to make sure that she's in good working order. The job is done.

Hints

- When you are positioning and pencil-press transferring the body tracing through to the easy-to-carve wood, make sure that the direction of the grain runs from the tail through to the nose.
- If you like the idea of the toy, but are not so happy with whittling, then you could modify the design and make the body from layers of plywood.
- If you only have $1/4$-inch-thick plywood, consider building the legs up from four thicknesses.
- The two between-feet dowels are important in that not only do they keep the feet apart and prevent the toy from twisting, but they also act as stop points to control the seesaw swing of the body when they come up against the arms and the tail.

11

Bill & Ben the Bowling Barosaurus Brothers

THE BAROSAURUS BROTHERS (bar-o-saw-rus), known by most circus high-wire aficionados simply as Bill and Ben, are ready for their act. The spotlight is on them, the crowd is hushed, and the drum roll is coming to a climax. And all at once they are off, rolling and spinning back and forth along the parallel bars. Amazing! Fantastic! What skill, what daring! The audience claps and roars.

Bill and Ben love the adoration and bask in the certain knowledge that they are the greatest dinosaur circus act of all time. But then, barosaurs have always been a big name in the dinosaur world. Ben remembers how barosaurus bones of the same age were found in both the United States and Africa, causing an uproar among dinosaur experts. This finding seemed to prove that at a certain period— about 193 million years ago—dinosaurs were able to walk across a single land bridge between North America and Africa. Bill and Ben have given it a lot of thought over the years. Could it be, they question, that North America and Africa once were really part of the same land mass? And as if being a big show-biz name wasn't enough for their egos, it was also on record that the barosaurus was big size-wise. Would you believe that Bill and Ben's great-great-great-aunt on their father's side measured, nose to tail, an incredible 90 feet!

Tools and materials
- A sheet of best-quality, white-faced, $1/4$-inch-thick multicore plywood, about 6×9 inches, for the two figures and the parallel-bar link pieces
- About 72 inches of $1/4$-inch-diameter dowel, for the two parallel bars and the two pivots
- A small amount of Super Glue fast-drying adhesive
- Eight colored wooden beads, $3/4$ inch in diameter, to fit the $1/4$-inch-diameter dowel
- A pencil and ruler

- A sheet of workout paper
- A sheet of tracing paper
- A roll of double-sided tape
- A coping saw with a pack of spare blades
- A workbench with a vise
- A hand drill with a 1/4-inch-diameter bit
- A pack of graded sandpaper
- A pair of pliers
- Acrylic paints in red, yellow, green, and black
- A couple of brushes—one broad and one fine-point

Looking and planning

The rolling, bowling, barosaurus toy (FIG. 11-1) is great fun! With the parallel bars suspended from the ceiling like a perch, or bridged across two chairs, or held by a couple of kids, or whatever, the spinning dinosaurs can be set in motion. And like all good traditional moving toys, the movement makes the rolling figures look as if they are powered from within. Of course, it's all done by good old dependable gravity and kinetic energy. By the time a rolling barosaurus has traveled from the top of the hill down to the bottom, it has gathered up enough energy to roll a

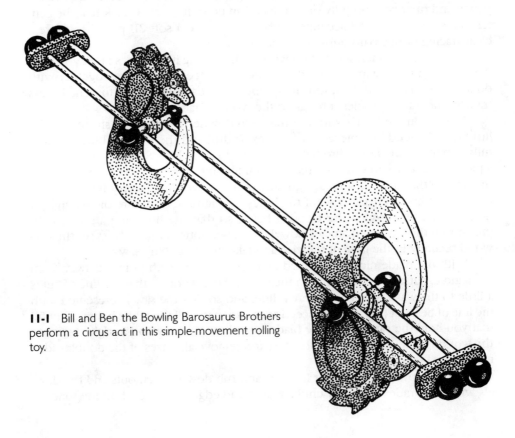

11-1 Bill and Ben the Bowling Barosaurus Brothers perform a circus act in this simple-movement rolling toy.

good way back up to the top. Of course, if the figures are left alone, they gradually lose momentum and come to rest at the bottom. The good-fun bit is that you can angle the bars this way and that so the momentum of the rolling figures builds up to a point where they are able to roll uphill. This toy is popular with children and adults alike.

Have a look at the working drawings (FIG. 11-2) and the templates (FIG. 11-3), and see how, at a scale of four grid squares to 1 inch, each barosaurus measures about 6 inches from the curve of the tail through the top of his head. If the spin-pivot is taken as being the center of a circle, the greatest radius is no more than 3 inches.

Note how the 3-inch-long spin-pivot dowel is glue-fixed through the 1/4-inch thickness of the body to allow both for the diameter of the parallel bars at either side of the body and the end-of-dowel bead stops. See also how the two 33-inch-long, 1/4-inch-diameter dowel bars are held 3/4 inch apart at the centers by plywood link plates. This project is beautifully easy to do—a bit of coping saw work and a few drilled holes, and you are three-parts finished!

Setting out, drilling, and fretting out

First study the design and the tools and materials list, consider possible modifications, and generally familiarize yourself with the way the toy works. Then take a pencil and ruler and carefully draw the design up to full size. Check that the centerpoints are clearly and accurately placed, then use a soft 2B pencil to make a clear tracing of one barosaurus and one link plate.

Saw the 6-×-9-inch sheet of plywood in half along its length, so that you have two pieces at 6×4 1/2 inches. Sandwich the two pieces of plywood together with double-sided tape (FIG. 11-4, top right), and use a hard 3H pencil to pencil-press transfer the traced profiles through to the working face.

When you are happy with the transferred pattern—the body shape and the little round-ended link piece—take the hand drill and the 1/4-inch bit, and carefully run the dowel holes through the wood (FIG. 11-4, left). Support the wood on a piece of scrap to prevent the surface from tearing as the drill bit exits, and hold the drill so that the holes are at right angles to the working face. While you have the drill on hand, check to see if the holes through the beads are big enough. If not, run the bit through the wooden beads so that the holes are a good, tight push-fit on the 1/4-inch-diameter dowel (FIG. 11-4, bottom right). Next set the plywood securely in the jaws of the vise and take up the coping saw.

With the blade nicely tensioned and set with the teeth pointing away from the handle, cut and maneuver both the saw and the wood so that the line of cut is a little to the waste side of the drawn line, and so that the saw is presented with the line of best cut (FIG. 11-5). Proceed at an easy pace, all the while being watchful that you hold the saw so that the blade runs through the wood at right angles to the working face. Ease the cutouts apart and remove all traces of the double-sided tape (FIG. 11-6, top).

Cut the dowel into the four lengths, and rub down the cutouts and the dowels with fine-grade sandpaper until all faces and edges are smooth to the touch.

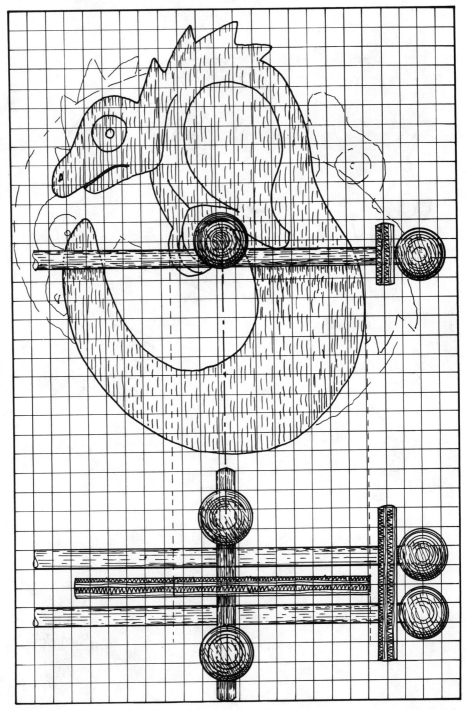

11-2 Working drawing. The scale is four grid squares to 1 inch.

11-3 Working drawing, design template, and painting grid. The scale is four grid squares to 1 inch.

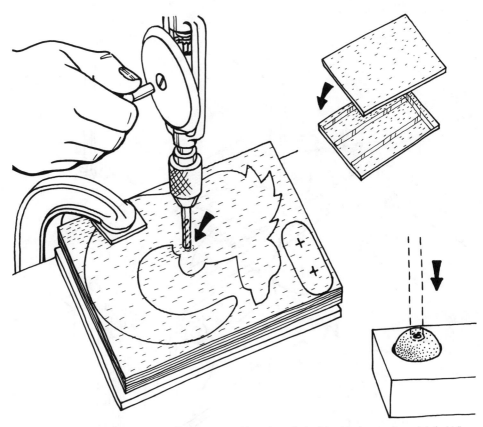

11-4 Sandwich the two pieces of plywood with strips of double-sided tape (top right). When you drill out the 1/4-inch-diameter dowel holes, support the workpiece on a piece of scrap wood and secure it with a clamp (left). Support the beads in a predrilled piece of scrap wood and bore out the 1/4-inch-diameter dowel holes (bottom right).

Take tracings from the painting grid (FIG. 11-3). Finally, pencil-press transfer the design details through to both sides of the cutouts (FIG. 11-6, bottom). Note that the only difference between the twins is that one is smiling and the other looks worried.

Putting together

Clear away all the clutter and set all the components out on the work surface. You should have sixteen items in all—eight wooden beads with 1/4-inch-diameter holes, two body cutouts, two link plates, two 33-inch-long dowels, and two 3-inch-long through-body dowels. Take the pencil and ruler, and fix the centerpoint of each of the two 3-inch dowels by measuring 1 1/2 inches along from the ends. Measure 1/8 inch out from each side of the centerpoint, and shade in the resulting 1/4-inch band with a pencil. Once you have marked precisely where the body of the toy is going to be fixed on the dowel, use the pliers to score the shaded area to pro-

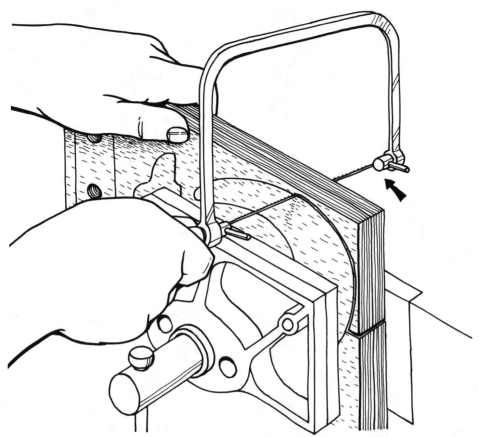

11-5 Secure the wood in the vise, and maneuver both the wood and the saw so that the line of cut is a little to the waste side of the drawn line.

vide a good key for the glue (FIG. 11-7, top). Then dribble a small amount of glue on the scored area, slide the dowel through the body hole (FIG. 11-7, bottom), set the dowel in position so that it is at right angles to the face of the plywood, and leave it for the glue to set. Repeat this procedure for both 3-inch dowels and barosaurus profiles.

While the glue on the through-body dowels is setting, slide the link plates onto the ends of the dowel bars, set about 1 inch in from the ends, and glue them in position. Glue all the wooden beads in place and have a trial run, just to see if the toy works. With the two dowel bars fixed so that they are parallel, and with all eight dowel ends protected with beads, the dinosaurs should be able to spin freely backwards and forwards.

Painting and finishing

When the glue is dry, wipe away all the wood dust with a damp cloth and move to the clean, dust-free area that you set aside for painting. Study the painting grid

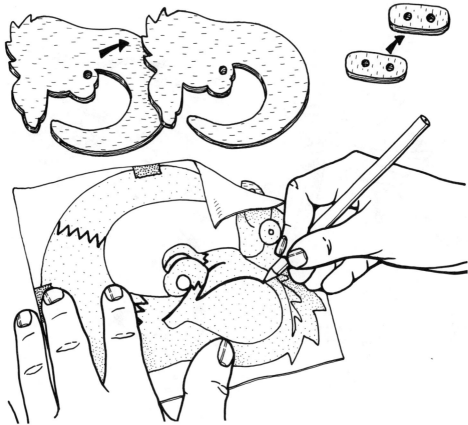

11-6 Ease the cutouts apart and remove all traces of tape (top). Secure the tracing with tabs of masking tape and pencil-press transfer the design details in readiness for painting (bottom).

(FIG. 11-3). Bearing in mind that the dowels need to be left unpainted, and the beads are already painted, simply hold the workpiece by one of the dowels, and block in all the areas of color that make up the design. For example, the parallel-bar link plate and the main body of the barosaurus can be painted bright red; the folds under the neck, the mid-tail, and the muzzle green; and the eye and the end of the tail yellow. If you need two coats of paint to cover, don't forget to give the work a light sanding between coats. When the ground colors are dry, use the tracing to reestablish the lines of the design. Then use a fine-point brush to pick out all the little black details of the faces and bodies.

Finally, when you have a well-painted and decorated toy, give all the painted surfaces a couple of coats of clear varnish, and the toy is finished. Now for the rolling and bowling fun!

Hints

- A coping saw is an easy tool to use, but only if the workpiece is held firmly and securely. Once the piece is held securely in the vise, reduce vibration by

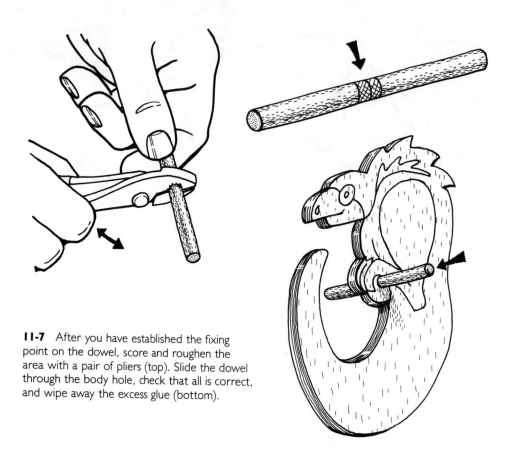

11-7 After you have established the fixing point on the dowel, score and roughen the area with a pair of pliers (top). Slide the dowel through the body hole, check that all is correct, and wipe away the excess glue (bottom).

making sure that the focus of cut is as near as possible to the top of the vise jaws.

- The through-body dowel pivot holes must run through the wood at right angles to the working face. You could ask a friend to hold a try square alongside the hand drill, or you could use a press or bench drill.
- If you like the idea of the project, but would prefer to go for different imagery, make a stick and cardboard prototype to test out your new design.
- If you use Super Glue, you must make sure that everything is perfectly placed the first time around.
- To avoid getting paint on the dowels, mask them with masking tape.

12
Stanley the Stegosaurus

POOR OLD STANLEY—what a life! His only claim to fame is that, of all the dinosaurs, he has the smallest brain! Yes, it's on record in all the dinosaur books, that the stegosaurus—pronounced steg-oh-saw-rus—has a brain no bigger than a medium-sized peanut. Okay, so Stan is big, and he is beautiful, but that's not much consolation when your mind is completely, utterly, totally, er, blank!

Stanley thinks and thinks and thinks, but he still can't remember who he is, what he is, and where he is. Most worrisome of all, he can't even remember why he is walking round and round in circles. He can remember back to 1877 when he was first found in Colorado, and he knows that he was called "roof lizard" because his beautiful back plates looked a little like a row of roof tiles, but as for remembering anything else, his mind is one big, fat, empty zero. Stan pulls his hat tight over his ears and carries on walking slowly round and round and round. Maybe, he ponders, if he makes a concentrated effort, he might remember just what it is that he has forgotten!

Stanley carries on walking slowly around, all the while thinking deep, pensive thoughts. He thinks about what he had for breakfast, and about what he is going to have for lunch, and about the meaning of life, and about, er. . . .

Tools and materials
- Three 6-×-3-inch sheets of best-quality, white-faced, multicore plywood, 3/4-inch-thick for the central body, 3/8-inch-thick for the two side plates, and 1/4-inch-thick for the four wheels
- A 1 1/2-inch length of 1/8-inch-diameter dowel rod, for the pivot axles
- About ten small brass washers to fit the 1/8-inch-diameter dowel rod
- A small amount of white PVA glue
- Matte acrylic paints in yellow, green, red, and black
- A small quantity of clear, high-shine varnish
- A pencil and ruler
- A sheet of workout paper

- A sheet of tracing paper
- An electric scroll saw, with a pack of medium-fine saw blades
- A hand drill with 1/8-inch- and 3/16-inch-diameter bits
- A selection of panel pins ranging in length from 3/8 inch through 7/8 inch
- A small pin hammer
- A pair of long-nosed pliers
- A small amount of two-tube wood filler
- A pack of graded sandpapers
- A couple of soft-hair artist brushes—one broad and one fine-point

Looking and planning

Stanley the Stegosaurus (FIG. 12-1) is one of those wonderful little hand-sized comfort toys that kids just love to hold and fiddle with in those odd moments when nothing much else is going on. With his four little red leg-wheels, he is the perfect toy for brumming around the floor, across the furniture, over the bedcovers, around the dog, and over the cat. The good thing about Stan is that he's small enough to go in a pocket or in the glove compartment of the car. Stanley the Stegosaurus is strong, he's easy to make, his form is just perfect for small, learning hands, and, best of all, his odd little wheel-turning walk is exciting in the best simple action-toy tradition.

Have a look at the working drawings (FIG. 12-2), and see how at four grid squares to 1 inch (top), Stan is about 6 inches long and 1 1/2 inches wide. Note the way the 3/4-inch-thick central plate is cut away and flanked with the 3/8-inch-thick

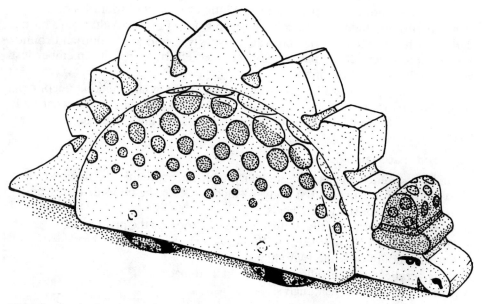

12-1 Stanley the Stegosaurus has pivoted wheels for legs, so he can be pushed along almost any surface.

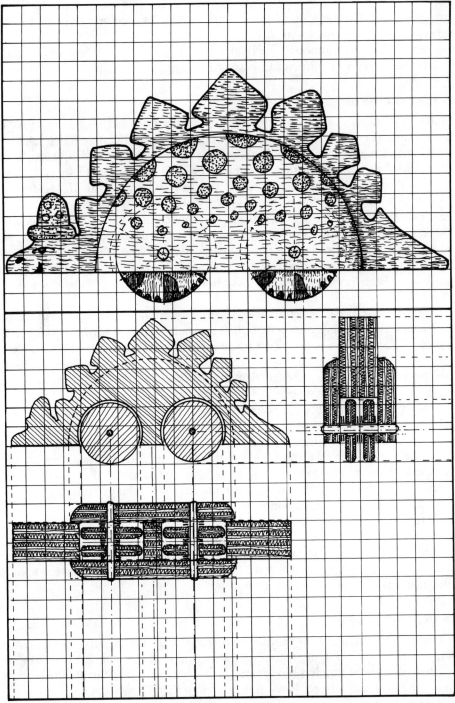

12-2 Working drawing. At a scale of four grid squares to 1 inch, Stan measures about 3 inches high and about 6 inches long from nose to tail (top). The cutaway and cross-section views at the bottom are not drawn to scale.

side plates, so that the four wheel-legs are set side-by-side and two-by-two, and nicely contained in two cavities.

As for skill level, although the final putting together is a bit finger-twisting, all in all it's a pretty straightforward, easy-to-make toy.

Setting out the design and sawing

Study the various designs and step-by-step illustrations so that you have a clear understanding of how the toy should be made and put together. Then take your three small sheets of multicore plywood and check them over for quality. With a small toy of this character, that is going to be held and probably sucked by toddlers, the wood must be smooth-faced and in good condition. If you find any problems with the plywood—loose knots, stains, delaminations, splinters, cavities, or whatever, then reject it and search around for a better piece. Some plywood types are so badly put together that they are almost impossible to cut, saw, and bring to a good finish. Whenever you are using plywood in a toymaking context, always use plywood described as best-quality, white-faced, and multicore or multilayer. Such plywood usually has about sixteen veneer thicknesses to the inch.

Have a look at the design templates (FIG. 12-3), draw the design up to the correct size, make a tracing, and pencil-press transfer the traced forms through to the wood. Make sure that you haven't made a mistake and transferred the shapes to the wrong thicknesses of plywood. To recap: You need seven shapes in all—the two large half-circle side plates at 3/8-inch thick, the single central body at 3/4-inch thick, and the four little wheels at 1/4-inch thick.

Make sure that the lines are cleanly drawn, then move the wood to the scroll saw. First of all, swiftly cut the wood down into seven easy-to-manage pieces. Do no more at this stage than cut to about 1/4 inch to the waste side of the drawn line (FIG. 12-4, top). Then take the pins and the hammer and tack together identical component parts. The four pieces of 1/4-inch plywood for the wheels can be pinned together, as can the two large half-circle side plates (FIG. 12-4, bottom). When you are happy with the arrangements, set to work with the saw, and carefully cut out the various parts. The saw work is easy enough with a toy of this size, because the thickest stack is no more than 1 inch. Using a medium-fine, well-tensioned blade, run the wood through the saw so that the blade is always presented with the line of next cut, and so that the cut is fractionally to the waste side of the drawn line (FIG. 12-5).

Drilling and shaping

When you have cut out all the pieces that make up the design, check that the wheels are nicely cut. If necessary, adjust the shape of the wheels by rubbing and rotating them on a sanding block (FIG. 12-6). Make sure that the axle hole center marks are correctly placed. Now, not forgetting that the wheel-center holes need to be 3/16 inch in diameter, and the side-plate holes 1/8 inch in diameter, support the layered-up cutouts on pieces of waste and drill the holes through (FIG. 12-7).

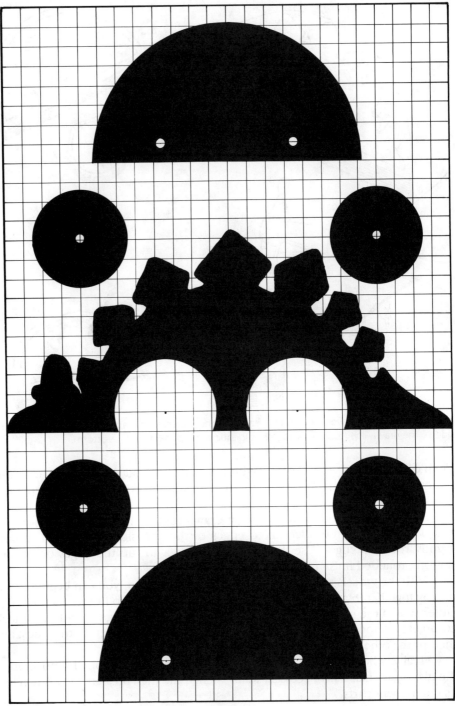

12-3 Design templates. The scale is four grid squares to 1 inch.

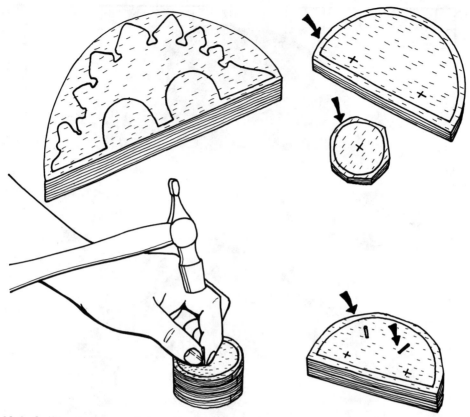

12-4 Swiftly saw the wood down into easy-to-handle pieces—cut about ¹/4 inch to the waste side of the drawn line (top). Tack together identical component parts (bottom).

Then carefully remove all the pins with pliers, make good the resulting holes and any other defects with a small amount of filler, and rub down with sandpaper to a good smooth finish.

Have another look at the working drawings (FIG. 12-2), and note how the wheels and the top outside curved edges of the two side plates need to have slightly rounded edges. Use the graded sandpaper to rub the edges down to a smooth, rounded finish (FIG. 12-8).

With the wheels and side-plate edges nicely rounded, you can begin putting the toy together in a dry run. The object of the exercise is to fit the side plates on either side of the central cutout so that the axle holes are aligned and the wheels are an easy, smooth-running fit. Pin one side plate in place, then fit the axles, and then fit the other plate (FIG. 12-9).

Finally, when you have achieved a good fit, mark in the precise position of the two plates, make any necessary adjustments, and then break the toy down into its component parts.

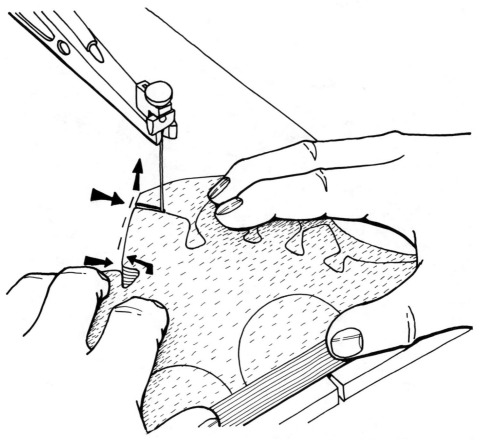

12-5 Run the saw blade slightly to the waste side of the drawn line, all the while turning and maneuvering the wood so that the saw blade is presented with the line of best cut.

Painting and putting together

When you are happy with the fitting, organize the area that you have set aside for painting so that all the tools and materials are comfortably at hand. Decide how you are going to support the wood while it is being painted. Are you going to hang it from a line, support it on a rack, or set it on little pin legs, or whatever? In this instance, you might find it easiest to support the wheels on dowels stuck in blobs of Plasticine modeling material and the main cutouts on pin legs.

After you study the painting grid (FIG. 12-10), stir the paints, and lay the colors on in smooth, well-brushed coats—yellow all over the side plates and central cut-out, and bright red over the four wheels. Be careful not to lose the alignment marks. When the ground colors are dry, paint in all the little details. Trace off the design details and pencil-press transfer them through to the ground color. Paint the green spots on the side plates, the green hat, the red spots on the green hat,

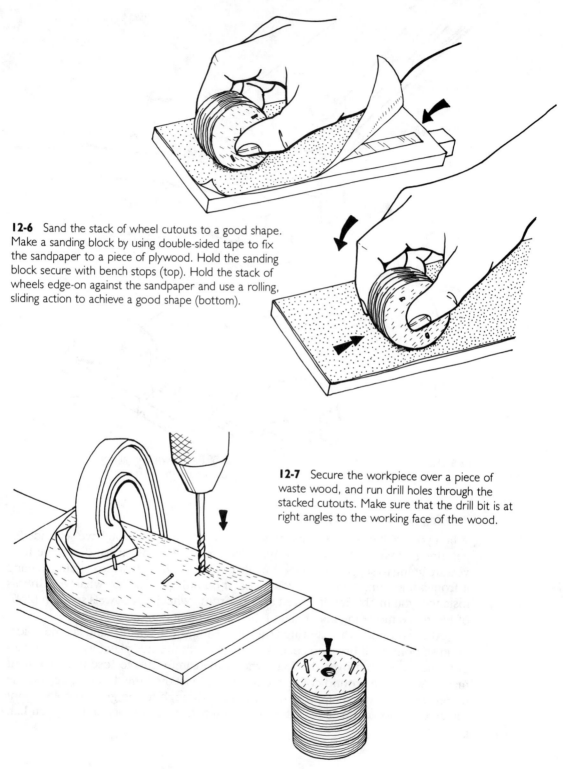

12-6 Sand the stack of wheel cutouts to a good shape. Make a sanding block by using double-sided tape to fix the sandpaper to a piece of plywood. Hold the sanding block secure with bench stops (top). Hold the stack of wheels edge-on against the sandpaper and use a rolling, sliding action to achieve a good shape (bottom).

12-7 Secure the workpiece over a piece of waste wood, and run drill holes through the stacked cutouts. Make sure that the drill bit is at right angles to the working face of the wood.

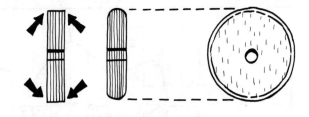

12-8 Use the graded sandpapers to rub the sawn edges down to a smooth, round-edged finish. To create the rounded finish, run the sandpaper from the flat face of the wheel over and around the edge (top). Sand the top edge of the side plate to a rounded finish, and label the inside face to avoid confusion at the painting and putting-together stages (bottom).

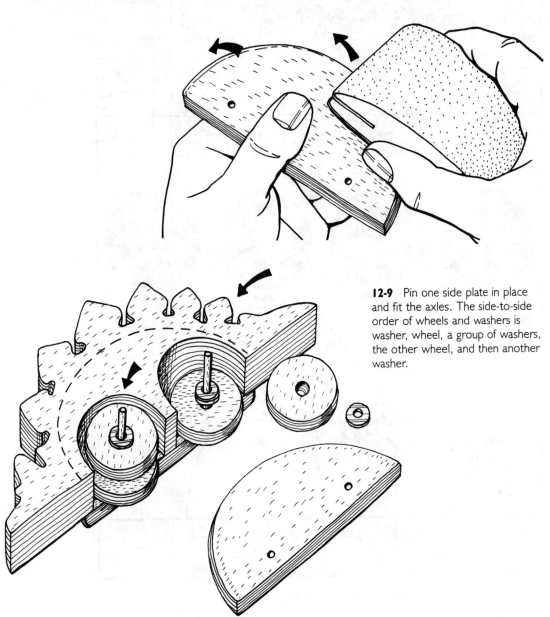

12-9 Pin one side plate in place and fit the axles. The side-to-side order of wheels and washers is washer, wheel, a group of washers, the other wheel, and then another washer.

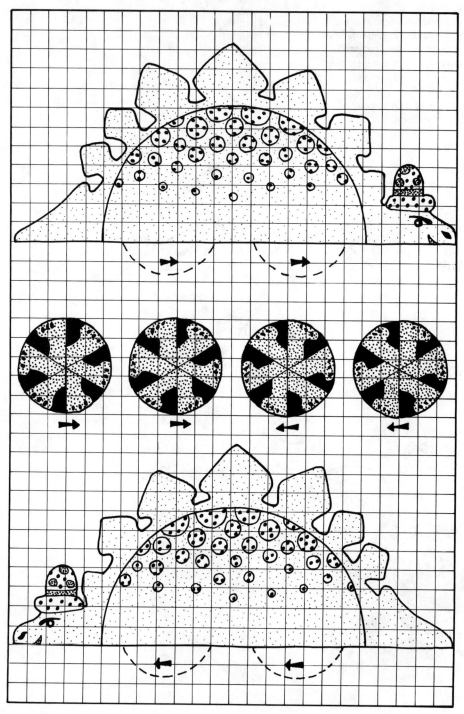

12-10 Painting grid. The scale is four grid squares to 1 inch.

the red mouth, and finally, the black eyes, nose, and feet. Make sure that you have all of the feet details pointing in the right direction.

When the paint is dry, glue and pin the half-circle plates on either side of the central cutout, set the wheels and washers in the wheel cavities, slide the axle dowels through the side plates, wheels, and washers, and fix everything with a dab of glue. Ideally, if all is correct, the side-to-side order of the wheels and washers on the axle should be a washer, a wheel, two washers, the other wheel, and then another washer. The function of the washers is to keep the wheels apart, and to prevent the wheels from rubbing on the sides of the cavity. When the little dabs of glue are dry, make good any scuff marks with filler or acrylic paint.

Next, hang the toy upside down from a line, with cotton threads around the axles. Finally, not forgetting to give it a light sanding between coats, give the whole toy two, or even three, coats of smooth, thin varnish and put it to one side to dry.

Hints

- You could use a single plywood thickness and work the project with a fret, coping, or piercing saw. All you do is use a single thickness for the side panels, three thicknesses glued together for the central cutout, and a single thickness for the wheels.
- While the varnish is drying, put up "Wet Paint" signs, and then friends, family, and literate pets won't upset hours of work.
- The painting area must be dust-free and well-prepared—no drafts, good lighting, plenty of newspaper over the work surface, and a good supply of old cloths.
- When you come to putting the toy together, make sure that the feet are pointing towards front.
- Special tip: Sometimes a dry, freshly varnished toy is so squeaky clean that friction builds up between moving mating surfaces. In this case, either wipe the surface over with a dab of wax furniture polish or give it a dusting with talcum powder.

13

Cedric the
Cycling Saltopus

CEDRIC SALTOPUS is one of those athletic types—all long, lean muscle and whipcord sinews—a guy who is always on the move. He isn't hunky in the sense of being able to arm wrestle with Rocky Balboa, and, at only 20 inches long, he isn't a potential Mr. Universe, but for all that, he is amazingly agile and fast.

Cedric comes from a long line of small, fast-moving, running, jumping, and leaping dinosaurs. Some scientists believe that the saltopus is the oldest dinosaur from Europe, perhaps even one of the oldest dinosaurs in the world! When Dr. F. von Huene first discovered a saltopus, in Scotland way back in 1910, he took one look at the delicate long-legged skeleton and immediately came up with the name, which means "leaping-foot."

But not for Cedric, a life spent trying to live up to his name—no way! Okay, so his father, and his mother, and his granny, and all his other relations had always run and jumped around, but was that any good reason why he should wear out his foot pads? No sir! The fact of the matter is, Cedric is crazy about cycles. He goes to his cycle workshop on a cycle, his hobby is mending cycles, he belongs to a cycle touring and racing club, he collects antique cycles, his friends are keen cyclists, he spends his weekends going on cycling trips, his vacations are spent cycling, and so on. Cedric eats, sleeps, and dreams cycles.

Cedric is ready for the big race. He's at his peak of fitness. His body is like a coiled, well-oiled spring. He's mentally alert and at one with his cycling machine. He's determined to win the trophy. Cedric arches over the handlebars and views the track as it stretches out in front of him like a long steel ribbon. The flag is up . . . the racers are under starter's orders . . . BANG! . . . They're off!

Tools and materials

- Three 6-×-6-inch sheets of best-quality multicore plywood—one sheet each at thicknesses of 1/4 inch, 1/2 inch, and 1 inch

- A sheet of workout paper
- A sheet of tracing paper
- A pencil, ruler, compass, and square
- A pillar drill with a countersink bit, and drill bits at diameters of $1/8$ inch, $3/16$ inch, $1/4$ inch, and $3/8$ inch
- An electric scroll saw
- Two brass round-headed screws, $1/2$ to $3/4$ inch long, with 4 brass washers to fit
- Four countersunk flat-headed rivets—two to pass through two $1/2$-inch plywood sandwiches, and two to pass through a $3/4$-inch plywood sandwich—with eight cone washers, four flat brass washers, and a tool set or anvil to fit
- A small ball-head or ball-peen riveting hammer
- A rivet set or drift pin
- A 6-inch length of $1/4$-inch-diameter dowel, with eight brass washers to fit
- A small saw
- A tube of Super Glue fast-drying adhesive
- Acrylic paints (we used black, white, yellow, green, and red)
- A small can of clear, high-shine varnish
- A couple of brushes—one broad and one fine-point
- A pack of graded sandpapers

Looking and planning

Cedric the Cycling Saltopus (FIG. 13-1) is a delightful pull-push plaything—silent-running, with a ingenious movement. It's a beauty! If you enjoy making small toys on the scroll saw, and if you know a child who likes crawling around on the carpet and playing with bicycles, a child who is excited by the notion of dinosaurs, then this toy could be a winner for you.

Have a good long look at the working drawings (FIG. 13-2) and the design templates (FIG. 13-3), and see how, at a grid scale of four squares to 1 inch, the toy stands about 5 inches high and 6 inches long, with a wheel span of a little under 4 inches. Look at the way the toy is made from four different thicknesses of plywood—1-inch plywood for the back wheels and the main body of dinosaur and bike, $3/4$ inch for the leg spacers, $1/4$ inch for the legs, and $1/2$ inch for the front wheels. Note that the two $3/4$ inch leg spacers are best built up from pieces of scrap plywood—say a piece of $1/2$ inch and piece of $1/4$ inch stuck together.

Study the cross section on the working drawing (FIG. 13-2, bottom), and see the fitting order across the span of the back wheels—a 1-inch-thick wheel, a washer, the 1-inch-thick body, a washer, and another 1-inch-thick wheel. The plywood spacers between the hips and the body are an important feature because they distance the various layers so that they are parallel, and so that they are all able to move freely.

The feet are set at 9 o'clock and 3 o'clock to give a good cranklike pedaling movement, while the cycle frame is pierced and cut away so that moving parts can be seen through it.

13-1 Cedric the Cycling Saltopus has a crank-driven leg movement.

Next look at the painting grid (FIG. 13-4), and see how the wheels are painted bright red and the jacket yellow and green check, while all the other details—the features and frame, are picked out in thin lines on a plain unpainted ground. The whole toy is varnished.

Setting out the design

When you have a clear understanding of how the toy needs to be made and put together, set out all your tools and materials so that they are comfortably at hand. Check that the plywood is free from loose knots, warps, stains, and delamina-

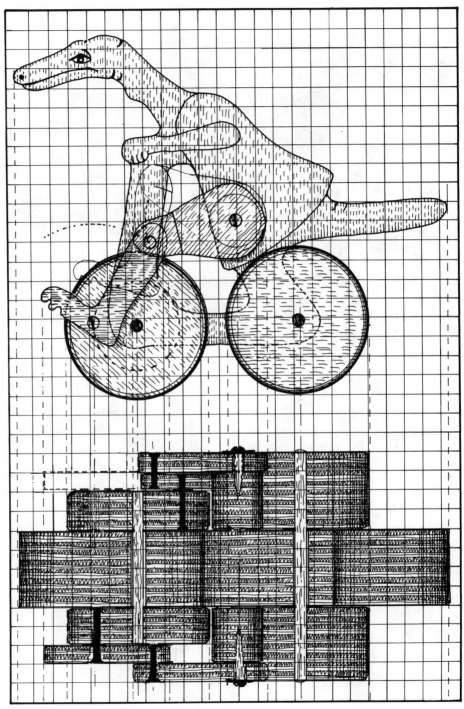

13-2 Working drawing. At a scale of four grid squares to 1 inch, Cedric measures about 6 inches long, 3 inches wide, and 5 inches high.

13-3 Design template. The scale is four grid squares to 1 inch. Note the ¹/₈-inch-diameter pilot hole in the cutaway window area.

tions. Next, draw the design to full size (FIG. 13-2), trace off the profiles (FIG. 13-3), and then pencil-press transfer the traced images through to the working face of the plywood. The main body of the toy and the two back wheels need to be on the 1-inch plywood, the two front wheels on the 1/2-inch plywood, and the legs on the 1/4-inch-thick plywood. Note that the two leg spacers are laminated to the required 3/4-inch thickness using pieces of scrap plywood. Make sure that the lines are clear, label all the profiles, establish the precise position of all the hole centers, and mark each hole with the appropriate drill size. For example, the two through-cycle axle holes are 1/4 inch in diameter, the knee and foot holes are drilled to fit the rivet size, the through-wheel holes are 1/4 inch, and so on. Don't forget to mark in on the cutaway area of the cycle frame a 1/8-inch-diameter pilot hole for the scroll saw blade (FIG. 13-5, top).

Drilling and scroll sawing

Support the workpiece on a sheet of waste wood, and then set to work with the pillar drill, boring out the holes to the correct diameters.

When you have all the holes bored out, move the wood to the scroll saw, swiftly cut the wood down into its manageable component parts, and then start to fret out the various profiles. The work is all straightforward as long as you follow three rules of thumb—work a little to the waste side of the drawn line, make sure that the blade is correctly tensioned, and check that the table is set so that the cut runs through the sheet of wood at right angles to the working face.

Run the wood into the blade at a steady, controlled pace, all the while maneuvering and changing tack so that the blade is presented with the line of next cut. When you come to fret out the window of waste on the cycle frame, unhitch the saw blade, pass it through the pilot hole, refit and retension the blade, and then cut out the waste (FIG. 13-5, bottom). Of course, to remove the workpiece, you just reverse the procedure and unhitch the blade.

Finally, when you have fretted out all the profiles, spread them out across the work surface and pencil mark the best face of each cutout so that you know what goes where.

Rubbing down

After you have fretted, drilled, and labeled all the plywood components, take the graded sandpapers and rub the cutouts down to a good, smooth finish. The cycle, dinosaur body, and limbs are easy enough—all you do is support the sandpaper in the palm of your hand and rub down the sharp edges. The wheels are a little more tricky, but only because you need to turn the workpiece as you sand it. Support the wheels in the vise and stroke the edge with the sanding block (FIG. 13-6, top). Use a sanding block or stick for the best results. Work with a gentle, rhythmic stroke, all the while keeping the piece rotating evenly while you are sanding. Continue rubbing down until all faces, sawn edges, and holes have been worked to a smooth finish. If you need to, repair damaged edges with filler and sand back to a good finish (FIG. 13-6, bottom). Finally, glue up the 3/4-inch leg spacers from a piece each of 1/4- and 1/2-inch-thick scrap plywood.

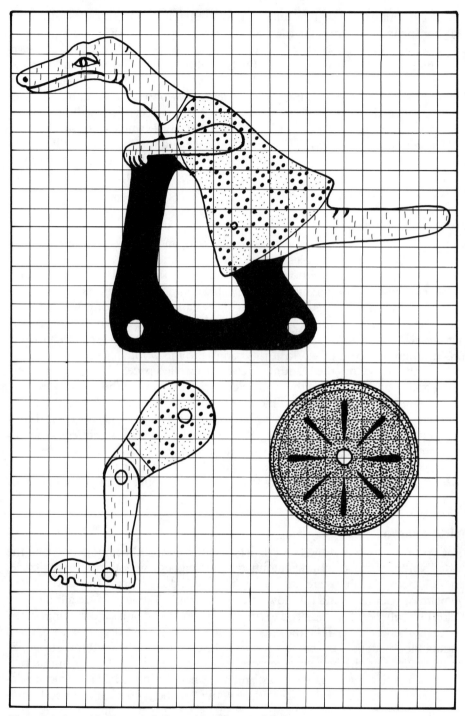

13-4 Painting grid. The scale is four grid squares to 1 inch.

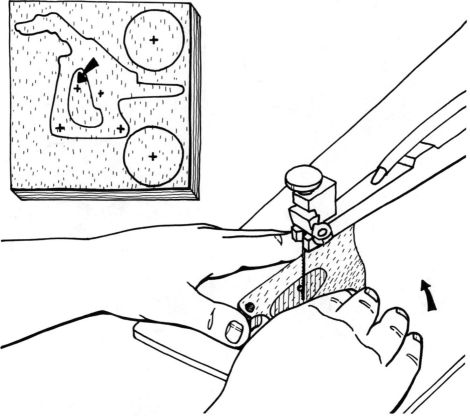

13-5 On the window area of the cycle frame, mark in a ⅛-inch-diameter hole for the scroll saw blade (top). Unhitch the saw blade, pass it through the pilot hole, refit the blade, and cut out the waste (bottom).

Painting and varnishing

When you have cut, drilled, and sanded all the components to a good, smooth finish, wipe away all the dust and debris, and move to the area that you have set aside for painting. Study the painting grid (FIG. 13-4), set out the paints, varnish and brushes, cover the work surface with newspaper, and generally spend time preparing the working area. (See **painting** in the glossary.) Start by giving all the components a swift coat of varnish. Be sure to brush away all the runs and dribbles.

When the varnish is dry, give the wheels a very light sanding and paint them red. Pencil-press transfer the various design features of each piece through to the wood—the eyes, the mouth, the cut of the coat, the pattern on the coat and trousers, the crease marks on the neck and tail, the hands, and all the other details. Then take the fine-point brush and the acrylic paints, and paint in the design. The cycle frame, the wheel spokes, and the dinosaur details are black, the jacket and

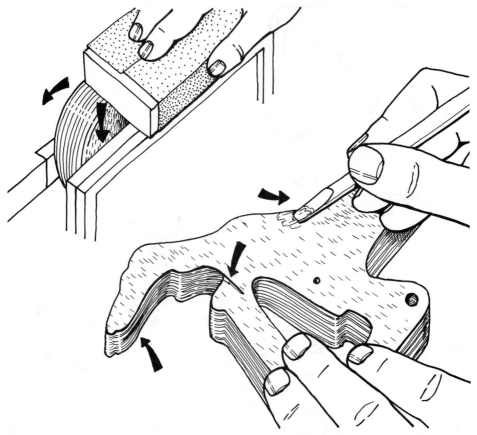

13-6 Support the wheel in the vise and stroke the edge with sanding block, repositioning the wheel in the vise as you progress around the edge (top). Fill any damaged areas on the surface and in the laminations on the cut edge (bottom).

trousers checkered yellow and green, the shirt white, and so on. To create the checkered pattern, paint the jacket and trousers allover yellow, and then paint the green check lines on top. If you have a fancy to give the dinosaur a name and number, or a spotted cravat, or a kilt, or whatever, then now's your chance to do just that. Paint both sides of the toy. When the paint is completely dry, give all the components another coat of varnish and leave them to dry.

Putting together and finishing

When the varnish is dry, you'll tackle the good-fun but tricky task of putting the toy together. First check that all the drilled holes are clean and free from paint and varnish. Set out all the components so that they are in an ordered arrangement across your work surface. You should have two 1/2-inch-thick front wheels, two 1-inch-thick back wheels, a body-cycle frame at 1 inch thick, two 3/4-inch hip spacers, four 1/4-inch-thick leg pieces, two dowel axles, four rivets, two round-headed screws, and twelve brass washers to fit. Have a good look at the rivets to see how your particular rivet type needs to be fixed, fitted, and clenched. Then take the countersink drill bit and countersink the appropriate head-and-tail rivet holes.

Pair the legs up so that the upper leg overlaps the lower leg at the knees. Now, one leg at a time, layer up the knee joint: cone washer, plywood, flat washer, plywood, and cone washer. Check that the countersinks are on the outside and the cone washers are in place, and slide the rivet home so that the tail of the rivet comes through on the outside of the knee. With the head of the rivet supported on the little anvil, use the ball end of the hammer to sink the tail of the rivet into the countersunk cone washer. Use a hammer and rivet set or drift to tap the mushroomed rivet flush with the surface of the wood (FIG. 13-7, right). Bear in mind that although the knee joint needs to be clenched so that it has as little side-to-side movement as possible and the ends of the rivets are flush with the surface of the plywood, the joint also needs to be a smooth and easy pivot-fit. Repeat the

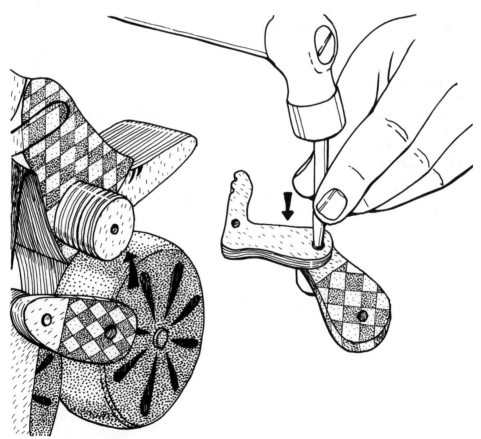

13-7 Use the hammer and drive or drift to tap the mushroomed rivet flush with the surface (right). Glue the leg spacer to the hip; then place a washer between mating surfaces and screw the leg through the spacer and into the body (left).

riveting procedure with the two foot-to-wheel pivot joints. With the four rivet joints at the feet and knees all nicely pivoted, take the two front wheels, two washers, and the length of 1/4-inch dowel, and set them in place on the front of the cycle. The fitting order across the span of the wheels is wheel, washer, cycle-body, washer, wheel. When you have all the parts in place, make sure the wheels are a tight push-fit on the axle, and the axle is a loose-turn fit through the body. Then turn the wheels so that the foot-pivot points are set at 9 o'clock and 3 o'clock, and dribble Super Glue into the axle-wheel joint. Wait a few minutes for the glue to set, and then rub the axle ends down so that they are flush with the face of the wheel. Repeat the procedure with the back wheels. Be warned—once Super Glue has set, there's no going back, so be sure to get it right the first time around.

When all four wheels are in place, use the Super Glue to fix the upper-leg spacers in place on either side of the toy. One leg at a time, glue-fix the plywood spacer so that it is set on the body at the point where the hip pivots (FIG. 13-7, left). Slide the brass washers in place, and carefully run a screw through the leg spacer into the body. Finally, repair any scuffs or nicks. At last the toy is finished and ready for the playroom, or perhaps for the executive desk!

Hints

- Bear in mind that the various moving parts must be able to slide smoothly, one in front of another. You might need to add additional brass washers between layers or rub down mating surfaces with a little wax polish.
- Rivets come in many shapes, sizes, and types. Most need to be clenched with a special tool or anvil. For this project, you specifically need a flat-headed, countersunk, flush-with-the-surface rivet with cone or cup washers to fit. If you have any doubts, ask a specialist supplier for advice.
- If you don't much care for plywood wheels, you could use plastic wheels or make the wheels on the lathe. See other projects in this book for details.

14

Pete & Pat the Pugnacious Pachycephalosaurs

PETE AND PAT ARE BONEHEADS! We don't mean to infer that their IQ is particularly below par, although, of course, their massively thick skulls do leave little space for brains; rather it is a statement of physical fact. Of all the dinosaurs, the pachycephalosaurus is credited with having the largest, spikiest, thickest head. Even the name—pronounced pak-ee-sef-a-loh-saw-rus—means thick-headed. The truth of the matter is that pachycephalosaurids in general, and Pete and Pat in particular, enjoy nothing more than a good head-banging battle. To this end, they have developed heads and skulls that are no more or less than massive, bony crash helmets.

Pete and Pat are pals. Their idea of pleasure is a good meal, a glass of fine wine, a Mozart symphony, and an hour or two spent bashing heads. Mmm . . . bliss!

Tools and materials

- A 3/8-inch-thick sheet of best-quality, white-faced, multicore plywood, 14×6 inches, for the control sticks, the bodies, and the legs
- A 1/4-inch-thick sheet of best-quality, white-faced, multicore plywood, 2×4 inches, for the arms
- About 8 inches of 1/8-inch-diameter dowel, for the pivots
- A small amount of Super Glue fast-drying adhesive
- Acrylic paints in dark blue, light blue, yellow, red, black, and white
- A small quantity of clear, high-shine varnish (you could use yacht or furniture varnish)
- A pencil and ruler
- A sheet of workout paper
- A sheet of tracing paper
- A roll of double-sided tape

- A scroll saw (we use a Hegner)
- A small hand drill with bits at $1/8$-inch and $3/16$-inch diameter
- A small quantity of two-tube filler
- A pack of graded sandpapers
- A couple of soft-haired watercolor brushes—one broad and one fine-point

Looking and planning

Have a good look at the project picture (FIG. 14-1), and see how this toy draws inspiration from woodcarved toys made in eighteenth- and nineteenth-century Russia. Or, to be more specific, you will note that the toy is very much like a toy known as "Muzhik and the Bear." Muzhik, moujik, or mujik means peasant, particularly in the time of the tsars. When the sticks are pushed and pulled, the muzhik and the bear take turns hitting an anvil or log with a hammer or an ax. Have a look at the working drawing (FIG. 14-2), and note the way the two dinosaurs sit astride the control sticks. They are fixed and fitted in such a way that their feet are pivoted to the bottom bar while their arms are pivoted to the top bar. The working action is beautifully simple and direct: As the sticks are pushed and pulled, the two dinosaurs take turns bobbing, ducking, and head-banging.

Note how the holes on the two control sticks are set in quite different positions. Unlike the other multiples—the legs, the arms, and the two bodies—each stick has to be drilled separately. If you are looking for an easy-to-make action toy, one that can be made and put together in the space of an afternoon, then this project is for you.

Setting out, fretting, and drilling

When you are clear in your own mind as to how the toy needs to be made and put together, trace off the design (FIG. 14-3) and carefully press-pencil transfer the traced lines through to the working face of the plywood. See the painting grid for

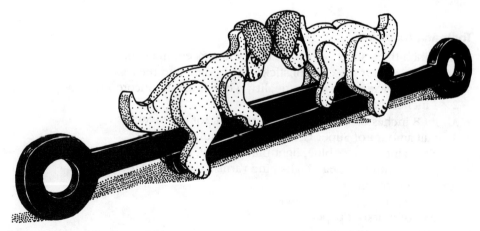

14-1 Traditional Russian push-pull toys inspired Pete and Pat the Pugnacious Pachycephalosaurs.

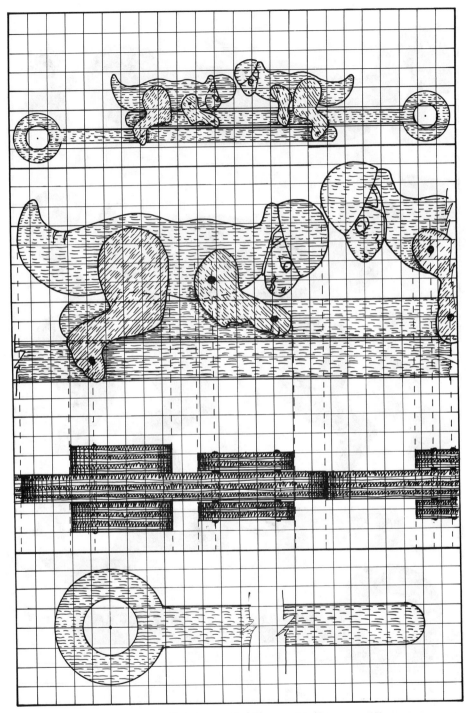

14-2 Working drawing. The scale is four grid squares to 1 inch.

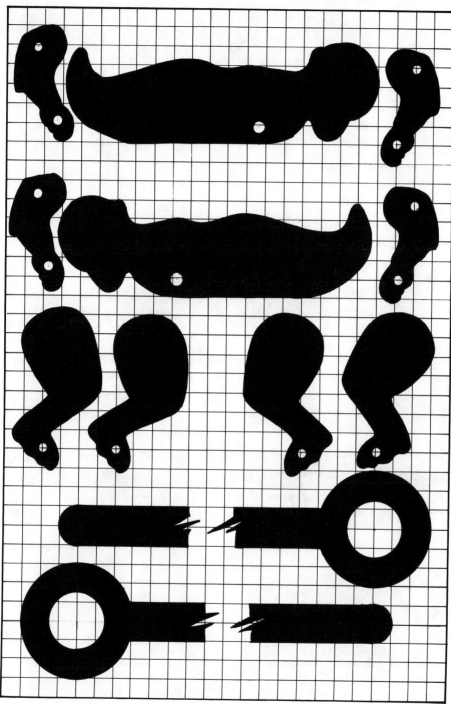

14-3 Design templates. The scale is four grid squares to 1 inch.

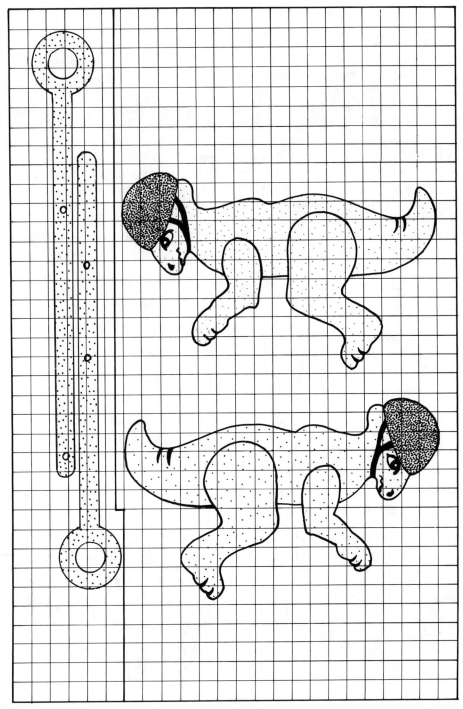

14-4 Painting grid.

the control stick profiles (FIG. 14-4). Make sure that the images are cleanly established, check that all the holes are clearly marked with centerpoints, and label the profiles so that you avoid mix-ups. When you have done this, move to the scroll saw and cut the wood down into easy-to-manage pieces. That is to say, swiftly saw around each of the profiles, with the line of cut about 1/8 to 1/4 inch to the waste side of the drawn line (FIG. 14-5, top).

When you finish the twelve rough-cut profiles, group them according to type, then take the double-sided tape and layer them up in stacks or sandwiches (FIG. 14-5, bottom left). For example, all the arms will be in one group, all the legs in another, and so on. When you are arranging the stacks, make sure that a good, clean pencil-drawn image is uppermost. Check to make sure that you haven't made any mess-ups, then switch on the scroll saw and set to work carefully fretting out the multilayer stacks. Work at a steady easy pace, making sure that while you are holding the workpiece firmly down on the saw table, you are also running it into the saw so that the blade is presented with the line of next cut. Bear in mind that if you go too fast the cut line will be ragged and torn, and if you go too slow

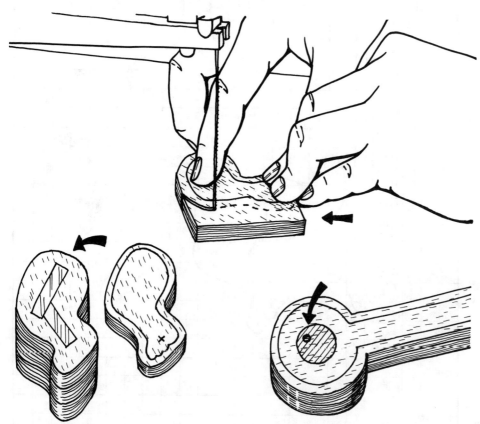

14-5 Swiftly saw around each profile to cut it away from the main body of the wood (top). Group the profiles according to shape and sandwich them together with double-sided tape (bottom left). Bore pilot holes through the waste windows on the control sticks (bottom right).

the cut line will be scorched and indecisive. Try to match the speed at which you push the work into the saw with the thickness of the wood. If you are a beginner, have a tryout on some scrap wood. Before you cut the control sticks, drill a pilot hole through the little round window of waste on the handle. Then unhitch the saw blade, pass it through the hole and cut away the waste (FIG. 14-5, bottom right).

When you have fretted out the stacks, take the two control sticks and very carefully ease them apart and remove the tape (FIG. 14-6, top). Remember how, from stick to stick, the pivot holes are set in quite different positions. Label one stick TOP and the other BOTTOM, and mark in the holes accordingly (FIG. 14-4, left). The hand holes, on the top stick, should be 2³/8 inches apart, and the foot holes, on the bottom stick, should be 6 inches apart. With the position of the pivot centerpoints clearly marked out on the two control sticks and on the body stack, set the ³/16-inch-diameter bit in the drill and bore the holes through (FIG. 14-6, bottom). Support the work on scrap wood to avoid exit damage when the drill breaks

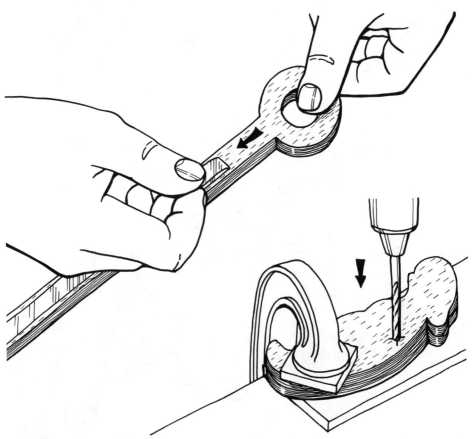

14-6 Ease the control sticks apart and remove the tape (top). Set the ³/16-inch-diameter bit in the drill and bore out the pivot holes, running them right through the stack (bottom).

through the bottom. Before you drill the arm and leg stacks, change the drill bit to bore out ¹/₈-inch-diameter holes.

Gluing

Have another close look at the working drawings (FIG. 14-2) and see how the back legs are fixed in position on either side of the body so that the dinosaur is able to sit astride the control sticks. Sand and reduce the inside of the bottom half of each leg by about ¹/₁₆ inch (FIG. 14-7, top). Use the tracings to establish the position of the legs on the body. Then dribble a good amount of Super Glue on mating faces and set the legs in place on both sides of both body pieces (FIG. 14-7, bottom).

Since the control sticks need to be an easy-slide fit between the legs, and a certain amount of paint buildup will occur, take the sandpaper and rub down the control sticks to reduce the thickness by about ¹/₁₆ inch. When you have achieved all the components that make up the toy, make good any damage with filler, and then take the graded sandpapers and rub them down to a smooth, slightly round-edged finish.

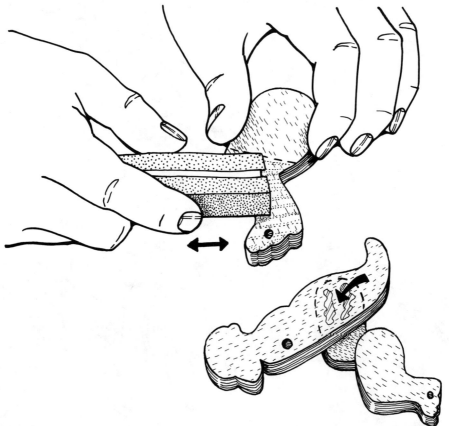

14-7 Sand and reduce the inside bottom half of each leg by about ¹/₁₆ inch (top). Glue the legs in place on either side of the body piece (bottom).

Painting

Clean away all the dust and debris and move to the area set aside for painting. Cover the work surface with newspaper and set out all the materials. Put up a knotted drying line, and make some wire hooks so that you can hang each component up by one of the pivot holes. Study the painting grid (FIG. 14-4). Start by laying on the main areas of ground colors: one body, with legs, and two arms yellow; the other body, with legs, and two arms light blue; both sticks dark blue; and both crash helmets bright red. Make sure that all pivot holes are free from paint. If by chance you need to lay on two coats to achieve a good dense coverage, give the dry paint a swift rubdown with sandpaper between coats. When the ground colors are dry, take a fine-point brush, and, one piece at a time, paint in all the little details—the eyes white and black, and the face, helmet, paws, claws, and tail lines black.

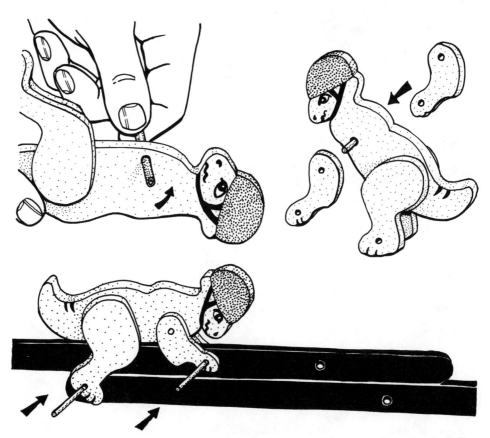

14-8 Use a small, rolled-up piece of fine-grade sandpaper to clean out the holes (top left). Pass the pivotal dowel through the shoulder hole and glue-fix the arms on the dowel (top right). Then pass the pivotal dowel through the legs and the bottom control stick; repeat the procedure for the hands and the top stick (bottom).

Finally, give all the components a couple of coats of thin varnish and put them to one side to dry. *Note:* Leave the inside faces of the arms and legs unvarnished.

Putting together and finishing

When the varnish is dry, you can begin the exciting, but slightly finger-knotting task of putting the toy together. Look back once again at the working drawing (FIG. 14-2) and see how, for a good, easy working action, the pivot dowels need to be a tight glue-fix in their holes through the hands and feet, but they must be able to rotate easily through the body and control-stick holes. Start by cutting the six $1^{1}/_{8}$-inch-long, $1/_{8}$-inch-diameter pivots to size, and cleaning out the body and stick holes (FIG. 14-8, top left).

Slide the pivot rods through the shoulder holes, and glue the arms in place. Have them carefully aligned and matching (FIG. 14-8, top right). Now, with the control sticks set in the correct position—one on top of the other—set the dinosaurs in place and push the bottom pivots through the appropriate foot and stick holes. Repeat the procedure with the hands and the top stick (FIG. 14-8, bottom). With the pivots in place, ease and adjust the limbs and pivots until the push-and-pull action is smooth and free. As a general rule of thumb, allow $1/_{16}$-inch space between moving parts. When you are happy with the fit, dribble a small amount of Super Glue into all twelve end-of-pivot holes. Finally, use a knife to clean off excess glue, and the job is done.

Hints

- Be warned—the placing of the pivotal holes is crucial. If they are out of alignment, the sticks will jam.
- It is possible to radically change the working action by modifying the length of the arms and legs and the position of the pivot points on the rods. If you want to experiment, make a working model with cardboard and pins first.
- If you want to achieve a super-smooth movement, consider setting brass washers on the pivots between the shoulders and the body, and between the hands and feet and the control sticks.
- If you can't use a scroll saw, then you might use a coping saw or fretsaw. (Refer to other projects in this book.)

15
Mavis the
Maiasaura Mom

MAVIS LOVES LAYING EGGS—splop! Out comes another, and another, and another. Splop, splop, splop, splop—a continuous conveyor belt of newly laid dinosaur eggs.

Mavis is a wonderful mother. As soon as the eggs are laid, she digs a depression in the sand and carefully sets the eggs in neat circles. When one circle of eggs is complete, she covers them with a fine sprinkling of sand, and sets to work laying more eggs and building more circles. Circle upon circle of eggs—one on top of another—until the 9-foot-diameter nest is full to overflowing.

Mavis was thrilled when Dr. Horner and Mr. Makela first discovered her nest building, egg-laying qualities back in 1979 in Montana. And, of course, she was tremendously flattered when the President awarded her the Best Mom of the Year medal, and she was delighted when the dinosaur hunters named her maiasaura, pronounced my-a-saw-ra, meaning "good-mother reptile." But really, she thought, with a smile, it was a lot of fuss about nothing. After all, what else could a loving, caring, maiasaura mom do with all those eggs? She had tried arranging them in lines like books, and in boxes like apples, and in all manner of fancy bags, bins, racks, tubs, and trays, but circles in sand were best!

Tools and materials

- A ¼-inch-thick sheet of best-quality, white-faced, multicore plywood, 24×24 inches, allowing for cutting and arrangement waste
- A couple of ³/₈-inch-long round-headed screws with washers to fit (brass is best), for the jaw pivot points
- A small amount of white PVA wood glue
- Acrylic paints (we used light blue for the dress, eyes, and slippers; yellow for the head, arms, legs, and tail; white for the scalloped trim and pom-poms; green for the polka dots; black for the eye details; and bright red for the bow and inside the head, mouth, and tail)
- A small amount of clear, high-shine varnish

- A couple of pencils—one hard and one soft 2B—and a ruler
- A sheet of tracing paper
- A sheet of workout paper
- An electric scroll saw with a pack of medium-fine blades
- A hand drill with a 1/8-inch-diameter bit
- A pack of 3/8-inch-long panel pins (brass is best)
- A selection of long, thin panel pins for the temporary pinning
- A 3-inch-long, 5/8-inch-wide blue steel spring
- Three 3/8-inch-long brass screws for fixing the spring
- A small pin hammer
- A punch
- A pair of pliers or long-nosed grips
- A bench hook
- A couple of soft-haired paint brushes—one broad and one fine-point
- A bag of marbles that are an easy fit in the 3/4-inch-wide channel

Looking and planning

Kids love Mavis (FIG. 15-1)—pop a marble in her mouth, and nothing happens. Pop in another, and again nothing happens. But after half a dozen or so marbles, the fun begins to start. When Mavis is full of marbles, then the marbles being pushed in at the top force the marble eggs out at the bottom. Just the sort of fun that kids of a certain age enjoy. Of course, it's all the more intriguing for young children because the marble that's pushed in is never the same marble that pops out. Mavis is a good toy for kids or adults. She's easy to play with and altogether good fun.

Have a look at the working drawings (FIG. 15-2) and design templates (FIGS. 15-3 and 15-4), and see how, at a scale of 3 grid squares to 1 inch, Mavis stands about 6 inches high, 9 inches long from her nose to the tip of her tail, and 2 1/4 inches wide across the span of the arms. Note how the toy is put together by layering, gluing, and pinning together a number of 1/4-inch-thick plywood cutouts. Note the way the channel for the marbles is created by having the three central plywood layers cut away and then faced by the outer layers. The same goes for the cavity within the head—the 1 1/4-inch-wide hollow is created by cutting away part of the five central 1/4-inch plywood layers and then sandwiching them between two outer plywood profiles.

Study the cross section of the working drawing (FIG. 15-2), and take note of the way the marble stop has been made from a short length of blue steel spring. Ideally the spring needs to be about 2 to 3 inches long, about 5/8 inch wide, with a screw hole near one end. We used a short length of an old clock spring, but you could just as well use a piece of steel crate strapping, or a piece salvaged from a metal ruler, or whatever. Just make sure when you come to positioning the spring that it can't be reached by small, nosy fingers poking in from the tail end.

Setting out the design and first cuts

When you have carefully studied the design templates (FIGS. 15-3 and 15-4) and have a clear picture of how the toy needs to be layered up and put together, draw

15-1 Mavis the Maiasaura
Mom lays eggs.

the design to size and use a soft 2B pencil to make a clear tracing. Make sure the
$1/4$-inch-thick plywood is in good condition. Hinge the tracing to the wood with
masking tape, and use a hard pencil to carefully pencil-press transfer the traced
design through to the wood. Move the wood to the scroll saw and swiftly cut it
into easy-to-handle pieces. Cut around the drawn forms so that the line of cut is at
least $1/4$ inch to the waste side of the drawn line (FIG. 15-5).

Grouping, pinning, and cutting

See how the toy is layered up from groups of identical cutouts—two head profiles,
five inside head profiles, two dress pieces, and so on. Then set the rough cutouts

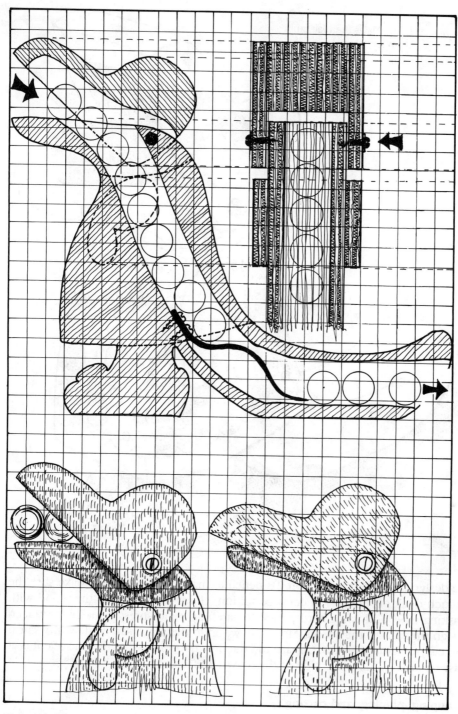

15-2 Working drawing. The scale is three grid squares to 1 inch.

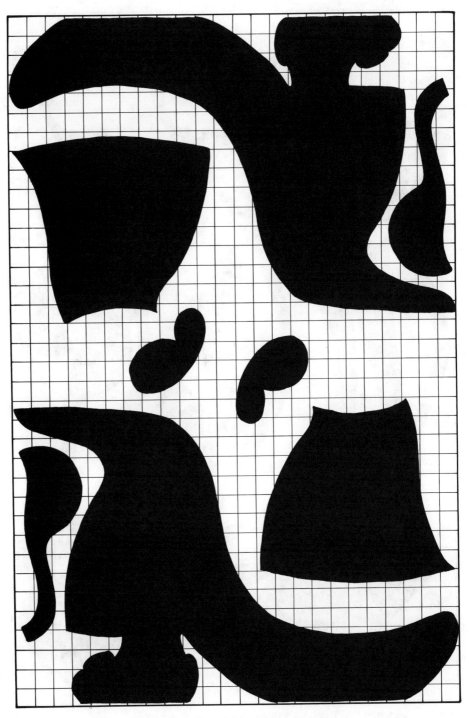

15-3 Design templates. The scale is three grid squares to 1 inch.

15-4 Design templates. The scale is three grid squares to 1 inch.

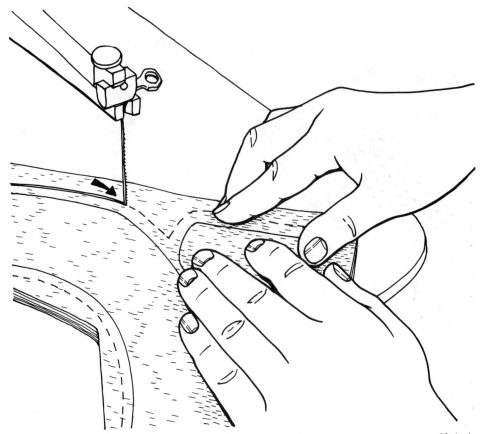

15-5 Use the scroll saw to swiftly cut the shapes out. The line of cut should run about a ¼ inch to the waste side of the drawn line.

in stacked sets so that one of the clearly drawn profiles is uppermost. Make sure that the stacks are arranged so that the sawn line will come well within each of the pieces, and then tack each stack together with two pins. The pins need to go through the design piece within the traced profile (FIG. 15-6).

After you have checked that the saw is in good working order, set to work carefully fretting out the various pieces. Using the scroll saw is easy as long as you follow these simple rules of thumb: Always feed the wood into the saw at a steady even pace, always allow plenty of time for presenting the moving blade with the line of next cut, and always make sure that the line of cut is just a fraction to the waste side of the drawn line. Cut out the two outside head pieces, the five inside head pieces, the two arms, the two dress sides, the two body-feet pieces, the three inside body-below channel pieces, and finally the three inside body-above channel pieces.

After you have fretted out all the forms, use the long-nosed grips to carefully remove all the pins (FIG. 15-7), clear the work surface of all debris, and set the cut-

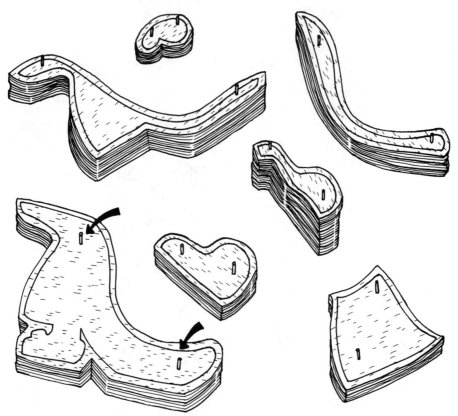

15-6 Stack the cutouts and pin them together. Place the pins within the drawn profile areas.

outs in groups. If all is well, you should have a total of nineteen pieces. Finally, label all the cutouts with a pencil so that you know clearly what piece goes where.

Fitting, gluing, and pinning

Start by having a tryout with the various pieces. Note the stacking order, and generally familiarize yourself with what goes where and how. Take the arranged inside cutouts, and carefully, two pieces at a time, smear a small amount of glue on mating surfaces, align the pieces, and tack them together with the 3/8-inch-long pins. For example, starting with the inside head pieces: If the five pieces were numbered 1 through 5, the order of work would be to glue and pin pieces 4 and 5 together, glue and pin piece 3 on top of 4, and so on, until all five pieces in the stack are glued and pinned. Layer by layer, take a hammer and punch, and tap the pin heads just below the surface of the wood. The work is all easy enough, as long as you make sure that the cutouts are perfectly aligned, and as long as you support the workpiece while you are working. If by chance you use too much glue, wipe away the excess as it oozes out at the edges.

When you have arranged, glued, and pinned all the inside cutouts, you next

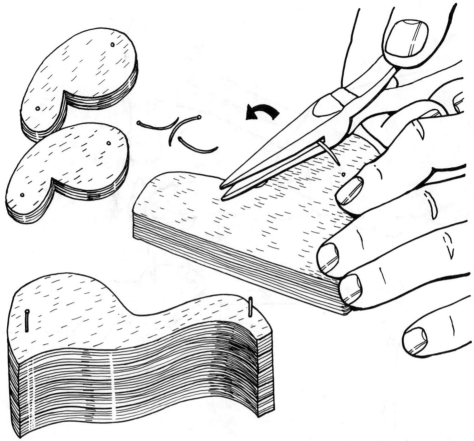

15-7 To remove the pins, hold the workpiece firmly down on the work surface, grasp the pins with the long-nosed pliers, and pull them out with rolling action.

must sandwich the inside pieces between the various outside profiles. Start with the head. Take the glued and pinned five-layer inside piece and carefully set it between the two outside face, or cheek, cutouts. When you are happy with the arrangement, pencil in across the width of the stack—meaning across the cut edges of the plywood—a couple of registration marks. Now, one side at a time, smear a small amount of glue on mating surfaces, check the alignment and fit, and fix with couple of pins. Again, make sure that the pin heads are punched just below the surface of the wood (FIG. 15-8).

The process for putting the body together is much the same as the head, the only difference being that because each side of the central core has three layers, the alignment is that much more difficult. Have another look at the working drawing (FIG. 15-2). Use the tracing to establish the position of the dress on the leg-body sides, and the position of the arms on the dress. Remember to make the features mirror images of one another. If necessary, sort out queries by putting the pieces together in a trial dry run. From one side of the body to the other, the sequence of

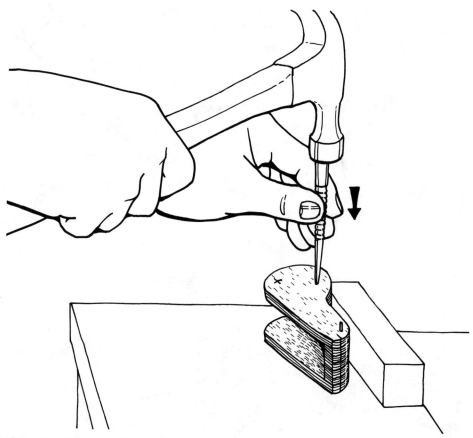

15-8 Align the registration marks on the glued pieces, and use the punch to drive the pin heads below the surface of the wood.

layers runs arm, dress, leg-body, central channel core, another leg-body, dress, and the other arm.

For the moment, put the two arms and the two dress layers to one side. Now, with one leg-body layer set flat down on the bench, position the channel core so that all sides and edges are aligned (FIG. 15-9, top). Take the length of spring steel, bend it to shape and decide where in the channel it should be fixed. You might need an extra pair of hands, or use temporary pins or a couple of small clamps to hold the layers in place. Make sure that the wood is thick enough to allow the length of the screws. Then take up the central core and fix the spring in place (FIG. 15-9, bottom). Next, hold the leg layers in place so that the channel is enclosed, bind it temporarily with tape, and test the spring. If all is well, when the channel is full with about six or so marbles, the next marble in line will put pressure on the spring so that a marble egg is released. Spend time at this stage getting it just right. If, for example, the marbles jam, you might have to move the spring along the channel—either up or down—or you might have to adjust the shape of the spring (the fullness of the curve).

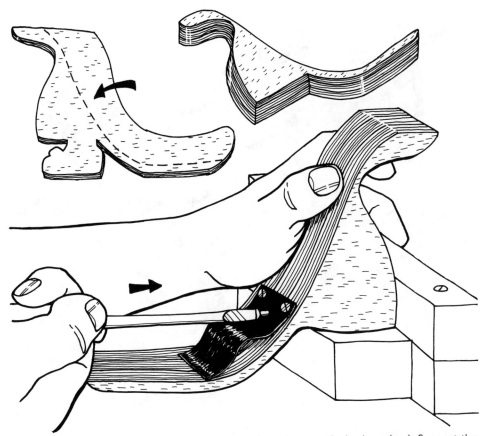

15-9 Align the side edges of the channel core and set them on the leg layer (top). Support the channel core and screw the spring in place (bottom).

When you have achieved a good movement of the marbles, remove all the temporary fixings and set to work sandwiching, gluing, and pinning. The easiest way is to start by sandwiching the central channel core, and then work outwards. Glue and pin the leg-body layers on either side of the core, checking that the feet are placed squarely so that the figure can stand upright; then glue and pin the dress layers on either side of the leg-body layers. Finally, glue and pin the arms onto the dress layers (FIG. 15-10). If all is well, you should be able to stand the figure upright on its two feet.

Drilling, finishing, painting, and putting together

When you are happy with the overall arrangement of the layers, slide the head over the bottom jaw and establish the position of the pivot point. Note that the top jaw is designed to clunk down on the bottom jaw (FIG. 15-2, bottom). Then pack the head cavity with layers of scrap plywood, take the drill and the 1/8-inch bit, and run a pivot hole right through the thickness of the head, in through one

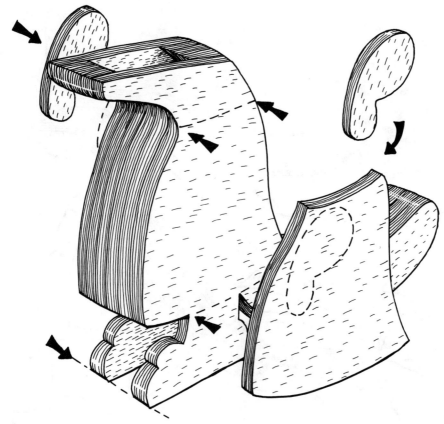

15-10 Glue and pin the dress layers on either side of the leg layers, and glue and pin the arms.

cheek and out through the other. Check to make sure that the bit is set square, so that the hole enters and exits at right angles to the working face of the wood (FIG. 15-11, top).

With the hole drilled, take the graded sandpaper and rub the whole workpiece down until all faces, edges, corners, and curves are smooth to the touch. Rub down and slightly reduce the mating surfaces at the pivot point—inside the head and on top of the body—so that the movement of the head is smooth and easy (FIG. 15-11, bottom). Don't forget to allow for the buildup of paint and varnish. When you have rubbed down to a good finish, screw the head in place and have a tryout with the head movement and the egg-laying action of the marbles.

When you have achieved a good fit and finish, take out the pivot screws, and move to the dust-free area that you have set aside for painting. Cover the work surface with newspaper, set out your chosen acrylic colors, hang some cotton thread on a drying line, and generally make ready for painting. Have a look at the painting grid (FIG. 15-12). First paint yellow on the head, tail, arms, and legs, then blue on the dress and slippers. Pencil-press transfer the design details through to the painted surface, and then apply white on the eyes, dress trim, and slipper

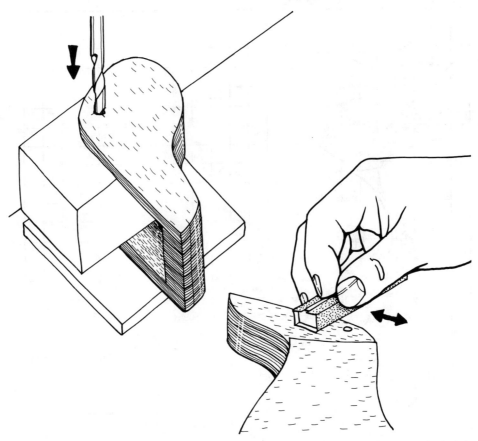

15-11 Support the head with scraps of wood and drill out the pivot hole. Make sure the hole is set at right angles to the working face (top). Sand and reduce the wood at the pivot point (bottom).

pom-poms; green details on the eyes, dress, and slippers; black on the eyes, nose, and hands; and finally a red bow on the dress, and red inside the mouth, head, and tail. When the paint is completely dry, give it a light sanding to remove blemishes, and lay on a couple of coats of varnish. Allow plenty of time for each coat of paint or varnish to dry. *Note:* For best results, leave pivot-point areas unvarnished.

Finally, when the varnish is dry, give mating surfaces a swift rubbing with a small amount of wax polish. Then pivot and fix the head with washers and round-headed screws, and the toy is finished.

Hints

- *Warning:* In the context of experimenting, finger-poking toddlers, just about everything is potentially dangerous. Toddlers of a certain age try to taste, eat, and suck just about everything that comes their way. You must somehow, without being anxious, get across the message that it's okay for dinosaur toys

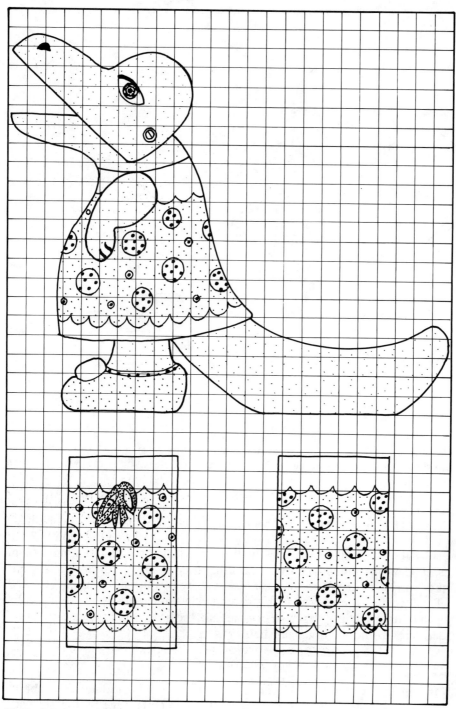

15-12 Painting grid with a side view (top), the front view of the dress (bottom left), and the back of dress (bottom right).

to put marbles in their mouths, but it's not such a good idea for children. The good news is that marbles tend to go straight through both dinosaurs and children without any ill effect!

- If you decide to change the scale and make this toy bigger, bear in mind that you either have to use bigger marbles or stay with the same channel width.
- You can simplify the design by leaving off the dress and painting the details directly onto the leg-body layer.
- When you are using the scroll saw to cut through several layers, the blade must be correctly tensioned. If the blade is slack, it tends to drift, and the cutouts within the stack will all finish up with slightly different profiles.
- If you use a fine, well-tensioned blade, the workpiece will leave the saw with a smooth, ready-to-paint edge.

16

Tracy the Tireless Triceratops

TRACY IS GAME for just about anything. Yes, yes, yes, she nods as she is pushed along. No matter what the question or request, Tracy always nods her head in silent agreement. Is she one of the largest ceratopsids? Did her great-great granny weigh in excess of five tons? Is she one of the last and most famous of all the horned dinosaurs? Does her name—pronounced try-serr-a-tops—mean three-horned face? Does her family have its roots in Alberta, Colorado, Saskatchewan, and South Dakota? Yes, yes, yes—she nods as she is pushed around the carpet.

Tracy really enjoys being trundled backwards and forwards across the floor. Is she very greedy? Does she eat a lot? Is her hooked beak useful for snapping off tough fibrous plants like cycads? Yes, yes, yes, she nods as her wheels race and whirl. Yes, yes, yes, she nods as her little cam clunks and clicks. Does she like kids? Yes, yes, yes, she confirms. Mmmm . . . , she muses, what could be better than being a little triceratops, and racing around the floor! Great fun—nod, nod, nod, nod . . . .

Tools and materials

- A block of easy-to-carve, straight-grained, knot-free wood, 10×3×3 inches—lime or jelutong are good choices
- A small piece of 3/4-inch-thick multicore plywood, 8×2 inches
- A 12-inch length of 1/4-inch-diameter dowel
- A 4-inch length of 3/16-inch-diameter dowel, allowing for cutting waste
- A small quantity of Super Glue fast-drying adhesive
- A sheet of workout paper
- A sheet of tracing paper
- A pencil and ruler
- A try square and compass
- A block of Plasticine modeling material
- A modeling tool
- A small straight saw

- A coping saw and a pack of spare blades
- A couple of small knives for whittling (we use small penknives)
- A small hand drill, with a countersink bit to fit the screw heads, plus drill bits at diameters of $1/8$ inch, $1/4$ inch, and $3/16$ inch
- A couple of small open-toothed surform shaping rasps—a flat one for general shaping and a tube for deep curves
- A pack of graded sandpapers
- A small amount of matte black acrylic paint
- A couple of brushes—one broad and one fine-point
- A small quantity of clear, high-shine varnish

Looking and planning

Tracy the Triceratops (FIG. 16-1) is an exciting, good-fun-to-hold, push-pull toy. The working action is delightfully simple and direct. As the toy is pushed or pulled, the fixed front wheels drive the axle, the revolving axle sets the egg-shaped cam in motion, and the moving cam lifts the beautifully sculpted head up and down on its pivot. The really good thing about Tracy is that she's so nice to hold and handle. All the forms are smooth and curved—just perfect for small hands. And then again, the wheel-driven cam movement is interesting—it's good fun to watch the way the revolving cam lifts the head.

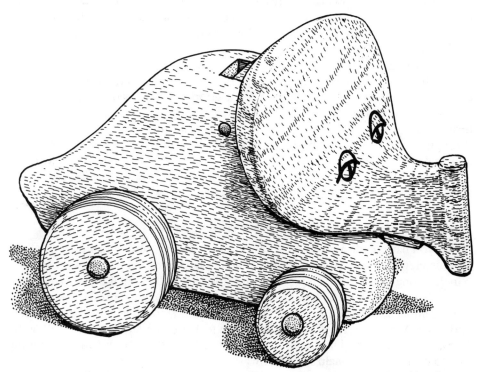

16-1 Tracy the Tireless Triceratops is a hand-held push-pull toy with a cam-operated head movement.

Tracy the Tireless Triceratops **185**

Have a look at the working drawings (FIGS. 16-2 and 16-3), and see how Tracy is unusual, in that the forms are beautifully smooth and sculpted. Note the way the wheels and cam are made from 3/4-inch-thick plywood, while the head and the body are whittled from solid wood. This project is slightly tricky, in that the body and the head call for a fair amount of free-form whittling. Once the overall shapes have been blocked out with the saws—the width and length of the head and body, the cam slot, the head curve, and such—then the final details and curves of the head and body are whittled and shaped with the knife. Of course, you will have a Plasticine working model to copy, but even so, by the very nature of whittling, you will have to be prepared to modify the forms and details slightly as you go along. The fun bit is, you can literally chop and change the shape of the forms to suit your own whims and fancies. For example, if you want to slim down the body, or cut zigzag ridges along the back, or give the face a fierce look, or make the nose horns more distinctive, or whatever, you simply modify the Plasticine working model, and then whittle and shape the wood until you are happy with the results.

If you enjoy making free-form sculptural toys, and if you get pleasure from whittling, then no doubt, this project is for you.

Building the working model

Study the working drawings so that you have a clear vision of how the shapes relate one to another, and how the various parts go together. Then take the block of Plasticine and sculpt a full-sized working model, or maquette, of the body and head.

First rough out the two pieces—the head and the body—and then model the slot in the body and the tenon-like projection on the underside of the head until the two components come together for a good fit (FIG. 16-4). When you have achieved what you consider to be a well-shaped form, use a long nail to pivot the head to the body. Make adjustments until the head moves freely up and down through its arc. Continue adjusting and modifying until all the shapes and curves that make up the body and the head relate one to another. When the working model is finished, put it within reach, but out of harm's way, and then clear the working area in readiness for cutting and shaping the wood.

Marking out the body and making first cuts

When you have made a maquette, drawn out the design, and made tracings of the various views, cut the 10-inch length of lime wood into two pieces, 4 inches and 6 inches long. Put the 4-inch piece to one side. Carefully pencil-press transfer the body views through to the 6-inch length. Thicken up the main profile lines, meaning the initial lines of cut, and then clearly label the wood TOP, SIDE, BACK, WASTE, and so on. When you have gone as far as you feel you need to go with labeling the faces, secure the wood in the vise, and use the small straight saw and the coping saw to clear away the main lumps of waste.

Start by cutting out the 1-inch wide groove that makes the through-body cam channel—the mortise-like opening that is designed to receive and enclose the

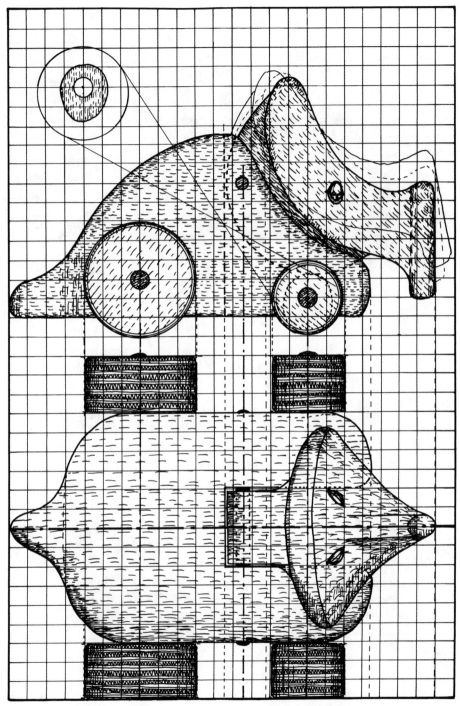

16-2 Working drawing. At a scale of four grid squares to 1 inch, Tracy measures about 6 inches long, 3 1/2 inches high, and 4 1/2 inches wide across the span of the wheels.

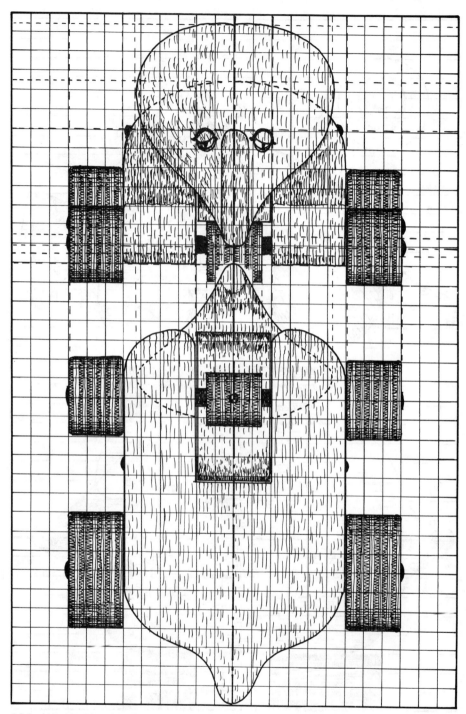

16-3 Working drawing. The scale is four grid squares to 1 inch. Note how the cam relates to the underside of the head.

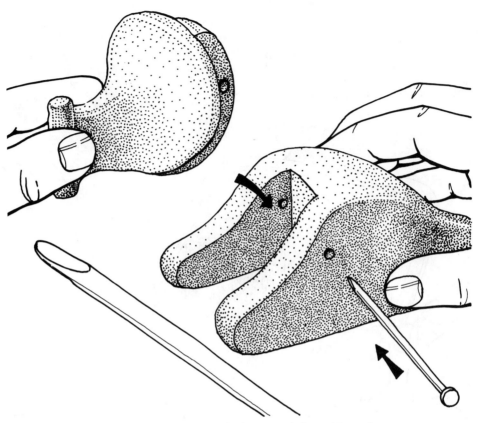

16-4 Fit the head of the maquette into the body slot and pivot with a nail.

neck and the cam. Use the straight saw to run two parallel cuts down into the front face of the body, and then complete the procedure by using the coping saw to link the cuts and to remove the slice of waste (FIG. 16-5). The opening should be 1 inch wide, about $2^{1}/_{4}$ inches deep, with a 1-inch-thick projection on each side. When you have cleared out the central waste—still working in plan view—use the coping saw to cut out the smooth-pointed shape of the tail. Repeat the roughing out, working from the side views to cut out the smooth-curved back and the front scoop.

Roughing out the head

Have a look at the design templates (FIG. 16-6) and the working drawing details (FIGS. 16-2 and 16-3), and see how the head is a tricky item to cut and work. Note, for example, how, from the side view, the grain travels from the front to the back of the head. See the grain direction arrows (FIG. 16-6). The neck not only needs to run down into the body cavity, it also has to be shaped along the underside to provide a smooth surface and an arc-like profile for the cam-lift contact. The same goes for the underside of the head and the cheeks. These details have to be cut

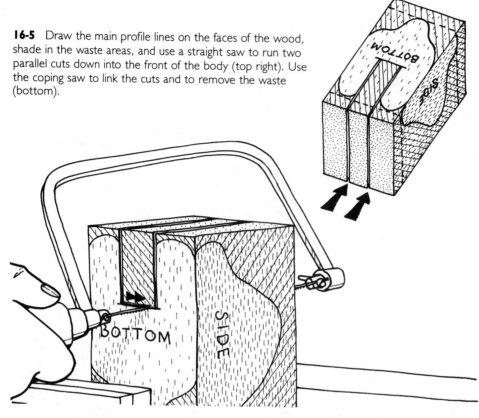

16-5 Draw the main profile lines on the faces of the wood, shade in the waste areas, and use a straight saw to run two parallel cuts down into the front of the body (top right). Use the coping saw to link the cuts and to remove the waste (bottom).

and shaped so that when the head is in the at-rest mode, it is nicely nestled in the front curve of the body. Work out the difficult shapes by studying your Plasticine maquette. Draw the profiles out on the 4-inch length of wood, labels the views, and shade in the waste areas that need to be cut away.

Start by using the small straight saw to slice out the waste at either side of the neck tenon (FIG. 16-7, top). Then use the coping saw to clear away the waste from the various views. For example, for the side view, you will need to run the saw from the top of the head, down the face, up and over the nose horns, and under the jaw (FIG. 16-7, bottom). Come to a halt when the coping saw blade strikes the curve of the neck on the underside of the jaw.

Continue clearing the wood at either side of the face, behind the head, under the curve of the neck tenon, and so on. Work with care, all the while referring to the working drawings and the Plasticine maquette. When you have cut out the blank, take the pencil and reestablish the main lines of the form on the flat faces. Finally, crosshatch in all the areas that need to be worked and wasted.

Whittling and modeling the body and the head

After you have used the saws to rough out the primary forms and clear away the main lumps of waste, then comes the much more enjoyable task of whittling the

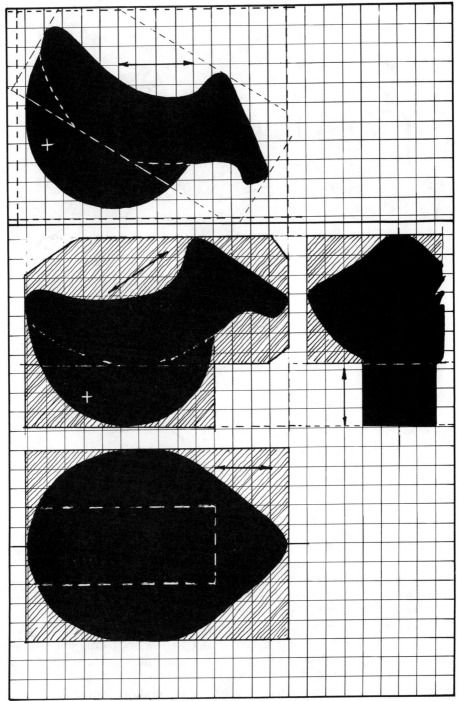

16-6 Design templates. The scale is four grid squares to 1 inch. The arrows show the direction of the grain. At the top of the grid is the side view as it relates to the initial block of wood; at the middle, the side and end views; at the bottom, the top view.

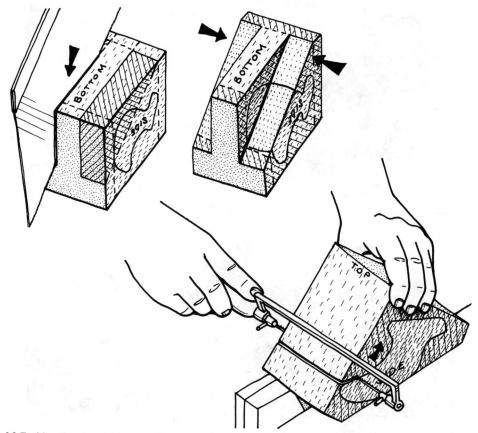

16-7 Use the straight saw to slice away the waste at either side of the neck tenon (top). Work the saw from the top of the head down to the face, up-and-over the nose horns, and under the jaw (bottom).

various bumps, dips, and curves that make up the design. With the guide lines drawn in on the wood, take the roughed-out body in one hand and the knife of your choice in the other, and set to work whittling out the shapes. Hold the wood as if you are going to pare or peel an apple, and then slice away the waste with short, thumb-supported cuts across the run of the grain. With one eye on the Plasticine maquette and the other on the run of the grain, whittle away the sharp edges and corners at either side of the body, until the back of the toy begins to take on its characteristic smooth-curved form (FIG. 16-8, top). Continue whittling, rounding the back and tail, cutting the curves of the shoulders, shaping and rounding the two projecting front pieces, and so on.

Every few minutes along the way, put the wood down alongside the Plasticine maquette and stand back and assess your progress. Ask yourself if the shape of the back is nicely rounded and hand-sized. Do the side curves run smoothly into the front and sides? Are you in danger of cutting too deeply? Continually

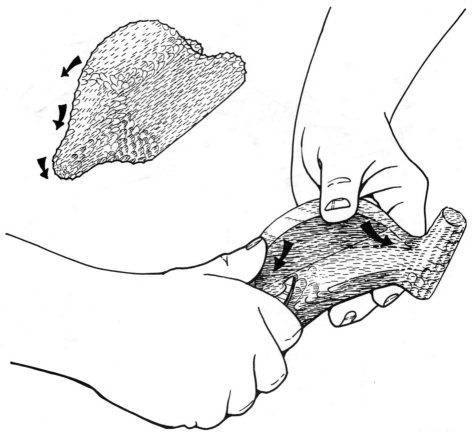

16-8 Whittle away the sharp edges and corners to create the smooth-carved form (top). Use the knife to remove the waste from the neck tenon, the nose, and the underside of the cheek (bottom).

checking and questioning your progress is important. Try not to concentrate on a single area—keep the wood turning and moving, and shape the whole form.

The head is slightly more difficult to work, but only because the deeply carved shapes run across the grain and need to be sharply cut in at an angle to the side of the neck tenon. Start by using the knife to define and model the flat side faces of the neck tenon and the underside of the cheek (FIG. 16-8, bottom). With the wood in one hand and the knife in the other, pare away the waste wood until the head and neck are a good fit in the body cavity. Be extra careful that the knife blade doesn't run out of control and slide into the comparatively fragile end grain on the underside of the jaw-to-neck tenon. Be ready to brake and pull back.

When you have pared the head and the body to a good finish, use the rasps to rub down all the facets and angles left by the knife (FIG. 16-9, top). Again, you will have to keep referring to the working drawings and the maquette. And just as when you were whittling, you will have to make sure that you are working with and across the grain, rather than directly into end grain. The rasp should leave the

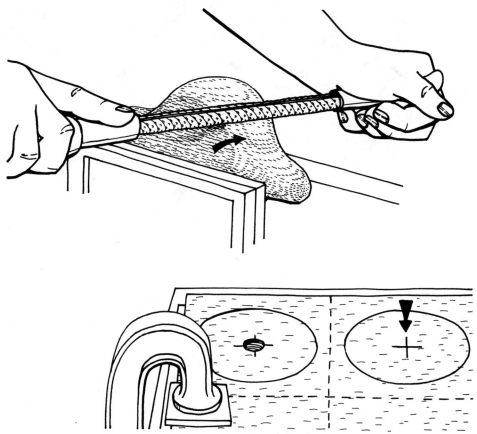

16-9 Use the rasp to smooth the carved areas. Work with the grain, all the while turning the tool to follow the contours (top). Having used a pencil, compass, and ruler to draw out the shape of the wheels, take the 1/4-inch-diameter drill bit and bore out the centerpoint axle holes (bottom).

wood looking crisply worked, with the tool marks smooth and shiny. If, on the other hand, the rasp cuts roughly, and the wood looks ragged, all you do is change the angle and approach of the wood or the tool until the cuts even out. Continue smoothing and turning, smoothing and turning, until you have what you consider to be a nicely rounded, good-to-hold form.

Finally, take the graded sandpapers and, being mindful to work in the direction of the grain, rub all the surfaces down to a smooth finish.

Making the wheels and cam

First, have another good look at the working drawing (FIG. 16-3), and see the way the wheels and the cam are made from 3/4-inch-thick multicore plywood. Note how the wheels are two sizes—1½ inch diameter at the back and 1 inch diameter at the front.

Use a pencil, ruler, and compass to set out the shape of the wheels and the cam on the working face of the plywood. Then take the drill and the 1/4-inch bit, and bore out the centerpoint axle holes (FIG. 16-9, bottom). Use the straight saw to swiftly and roughly cut out the component parts; then, one piece it a time, secure the wood in the vise and use the coping saw to fret out the shapes. The work is all simple enough, as long as you continually make sure that you hold the saw so the blade is at right angles to the working face. Keep repositioning the wood in the vise so that the saw is presented with the line of next cut, making sure the cut line is a little to the waste side of the drawn line (FIG. 16-10, top).

When you have fretted out the five shapes—two small wheels, two large wheels, and the cam—set to work with the graded sandpaper and rub the cut faces down to a smooth, slightly round-cornered finish (FIG. 16-10, bottom).

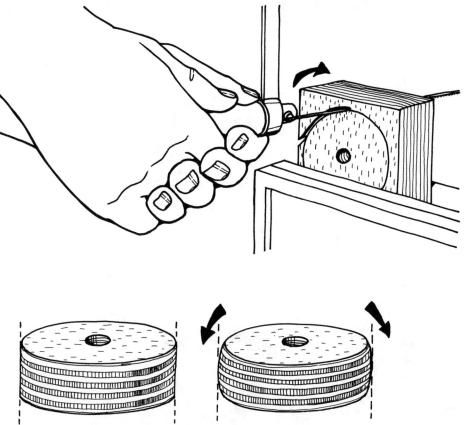

16-10 Secure the wood in the vise and use a coping saw to carefully fret out the shapes. Work to the waste side of the drawn line, holding the saw so that the cut face is at right angles to the working face (top). Use the graded sandpapers to rub the cut faces down to a smooth round-cornered finish (bottom).

Putting together and finishing

Set all the components out on the work surface and check them over for size, fit, and finish. You should have the body, the head, two small wheels, two large wheels, a single cam, two $4^3/4$-inch-long, $1/4$-inch-diameter axle dowels—allowing for a $1/16$-inch gap between moving surfaces and for the rounded axle ends—and a single 3-inch-long, $3/16$-inch-diameter through-body pivot rod. Note the way the axles need to be a tight fit through the wheels and cam, and a loose fit through the body, while the pivot rod needs to be a loose fit through the head and neck and a tight fit through the body. Establish the position of the through-body axles holes and run them through with the $1/4$-inch drill bit. Make several passes with the drill until the dowel is a loose fit.

When you come to repeat the same procedure with the through-body pivot, settle for one pass through the body and several passes through the neck. Run a $1/8$-inch-diameter hole through the cam so that you can countersink a screw. Have a trial put-together to check for fit. Slide the axles into place—the back axle

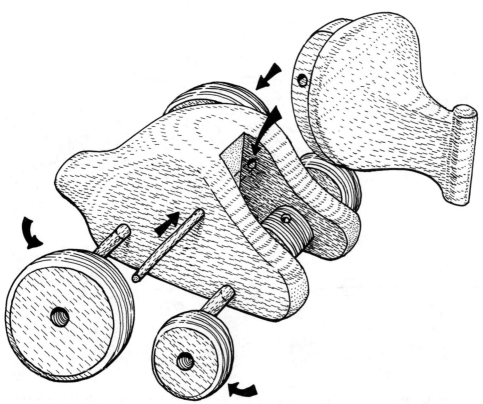

16-11 Have a trial put-together to check for fit. Slide the axles into position—the back axle through the body and the front axle through the body and cam—and push the wheels onto the axle stubs. Screw the cam to the axle, put the head in position, and slide the pivot rod through the body.

through the body, and the front axle through the body and cam—and push the wheels onto the ends of the axle stubs. Screw the cam onto the axle, put the head in place, and slide the pivot through the body (FIG. 16-11). If all is correct, as the toy is pushed slowly along—forwards or backwards—the cam will follow the curve of the neck tenon and lift the head up on its pivot. Of course, once the cam has moved out of contact with the neck, the fit of the neck in the body should be loose enough to allow the head to drop back to the at-rest position.

When you are happy with the way the toy fits together, rub the axle ends down to a rounded finish, pencil in the position of the cam, and then carefully ease the toy apart. Then take the fine-point brush and the black acrylic paint, and paint the eye details. When the acrylic paint is completely dry—don't forget to give the surfaces a swift rubbing down between coats—give all the components a couple of thin coats of clear varnish. Wait for the varnish to dry thoroughly, then dribble and smear a small amount of glue in the wheel and body pivot holes, and carefully put the toy back together again. Remove excess glue. Finally, touch up scuff marks with varnish, and the job is done. Tracy the Triceratops is now ready for her first action-packed trip across the rugged terrain of the playroom carpet.

Hints

- With a free-form project of this size and character, making a prototype, maquette, or working model is essential. If you can't use Plasticine, you could use clay, modeling wax, soap, or even flour dough.
- If you like the idea of the project, but are not so keen on cutting and working the head and neck from a single lump of wood, you could make the head one component and the neck a jointed addition.
- Although this project suggests that you use an easy-to-work, light-colored wood like lime or jelutong, no technical reason keeps you from going for a dark wood like mahogany. Think carefully before you use precious rare woods!
- You could speed up the project by using store-bought plastic wheels.
- If you like the overall concept of the toy, but are not happy about the whittling, the designs can be simplified. You could achieve the head and the body by building up layers of plywood and smoothing the contours with a surform. The exposed end of the plywood would make an exciting decorative texture.
- Be warned—Super Glue sticks very fast. Once it's down, you can't go back. Work with care.

A Toymaker's Glossary

acrylic paint An easy-to-use, water-based, quick-drying, PVA paint. Acrylics are good for toymaking because they can be used straight from the can, the colors are bright, they are fast-drying, the brushes can be washed clean in water, and, once in place, the paint is nontoxic. Since dinosaur toys get a lot of handling, protect the painted surfaces with a couple of coats of clear, high-shine varnish.

axle In the context of this book, an axle might be anything from a long screw to a length of dowel. If it supports and holds a wheel, then it is an axle.

bearing Any tube, guide, bridge-shaped block, or containment that holds and supports a turning shaft, an axle, or a pivot might be termed a bearing. Mating moving surfaces—where the axle passes through the bearing—are best left unpainted and then waxed.

blank A block, slab, disc, or cylinder of ready-to-work wood.

brushes Use flat brushes for varnishing; long-haired, fine-point brushes for details; broad brushes for large areas of flat paint; and so on. We use soft-haired brushes—sable or nylon—like those used by watercolor artists. Wash your brushes as soon as you are finished with them, dry them well, and store them with the heads tightly bound with plastic film.

calipers A two-legged measuring instrument used for checking widths and diameters. We use a pair that has a positive, one-hand screw adjustment.

cam In the context of dinosaur toys, a rotating, offset, egg-shaped form attached to the drive shaft. As the drive shaft turns, the cam sets some part of the toy in motion.

caster A small, swivel ball- or disc-type wheel, used to achieve an easy, smooth, stable, tight-turn movement.

centering and roughing out The process of mounting the wood on the lathe and swiftly turning the wood down to the initial ready-to-work cylinder. Starting with a square length of wood, the working stages are:
1. Establish the end centerpoints by drawing crossed diagonals.
2. Locate, or spike, the wood onto the pronged drive or headstock center.

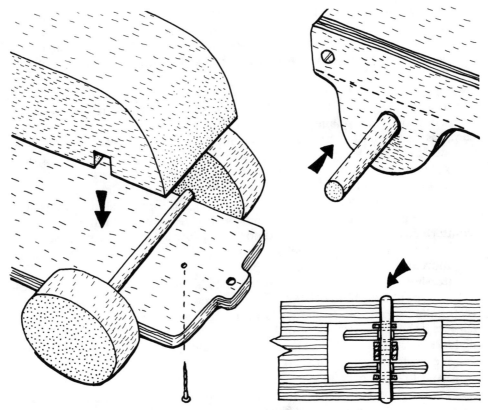

Axles One type of axle is fixed to the wheels, and is a loose fit between the car body and the base (left). Another type is fixed to the wheels (not shown) and moves freely in the holes in the side plates, which are screwed to the sides of the chassis (top right). A third axle is fixed, with the wheels free to turn on the axle (bottom right).

3. Bring the tailstock up towards the work and clamp it into position.
4. Wind the tailstock center into the wood.
5. Fix the tool rest just below center height so that it is clear of the work, and test for an unobstructed swing.
6. Grasp the tool in both hands and brace it on the rest.
7. Switch on the power and run the tool backwards and forwards along the wood until the initial cylinder is roughed out.

Note: If you are working on a small lathe, cut the wood down to an octagonal section before mounting it on the lathe. See **roughing out.**

centerline One or more lines that mark out the center of a symmetrical form or image. Sometimes two such lines—one that runs from side to side, and another that runs from front to back—cross each other at right angles.

chuck In the context of woodturning on a large lathe, a four-jaw chuck is a beautifully efficient and time-saving piece of equipment that holds and grips the workpiece while it is being turned. In use, the four jaws are screwed in geared unison towards the center, to grip and centralize the workpiece.

clamps, cramps, and holdfasts Devices used for holding the workpiece secure while it is being worked. You can use G-clamps, C-clamps, strap clamps, hold-downs, holdfasts, and so on. Protect the workpiece by setting an offcut piece of waste between it and the jaws or head of the holdfast or clamp. See **V-block**.

close-grained Describes wood that has regularly spaced annual rings. For small toys that are going to be cuddled and sucked, always make sure that your chosen wood is also splinter-proof and nontoxic.

compass A two-legged, hand-held instrument used for drawing circles and arcs. We use a long-legged, multipurpose, screw-operated compass with a pen-holding attachment and an extension arm. See **dividers**.

coping saw A small, flexible-bladed frame saw used for cutting curves, holes, and profiles in thin wood. A coping saw is good for toymaking because the inexpensive, pin-ended blades can be swiftly removed and refitted.

counterbalance Many of the small dinosaur toys use a counterbalance, usually in the form of a seesaw-like weight or extension that balances or offsets another movement.

countersink To enlarge the upper part of a hole, making a cone-shaped depression, so that the head of a bolt, rivet, or screw can be sunk below the surface.

craft knife A knife with a short, sharp, strong, easy-to-change blade.

cutouts The sawn shapes that make up the project.

dividers A two-legged, compass-like instrument used for stepping off measurements. In the context of woodturning, heavy-duty, knifepoint dividers are fixed to a set measurement and held against the workpiece while it is in motion. The points mark the surface with small, V-groove cuts. *Warning:* Beginners should stop the lathe when using dividers.

double-sided tape A tape that is sticky on both sides; good for holding pieces of plywood together while cutting out identical multiple shapes on the scroll saw.

dowel or rod Storebought, ready-to-use, round-section wood, one of the toymaker's primary materials. Dowel is sold in diameters that range from 1/8 inch through 1 inch. Dowel can be used as axle rods, sliced to make wheels, cut and carved for limbs, used for glue-peg fixing, and so on.

drilling holes The act of boring, sinking, or running holes through the workpiece. Depending upon the job in hand, we use a hand-held electric drill, a bench or press drill, or a small wind-and-turn hand drill. Before drilling, back the workpiece with a scrap of wood and secure it with a clamp and check the angle of the drill by eye or with a try square. Hold and steady the drill with one hand and set it in motion with the other.

dust-free Wood dust can irritate the skin and damage the eyes, ears, nose, and throat. Some woodworkers prefer to wear a mask. Prior to painting or varnishing, make sure that the workpiece and work surfaces are completely free from wood dust. Sweep up debris, vacuum surfaces, and then wipe the workpiece over with a damp cloth. Ideally, you should paint in a dust-free area that you have set aside for that purpose.

files Files come in many shapes and sizes, from fine needle and riffler files to

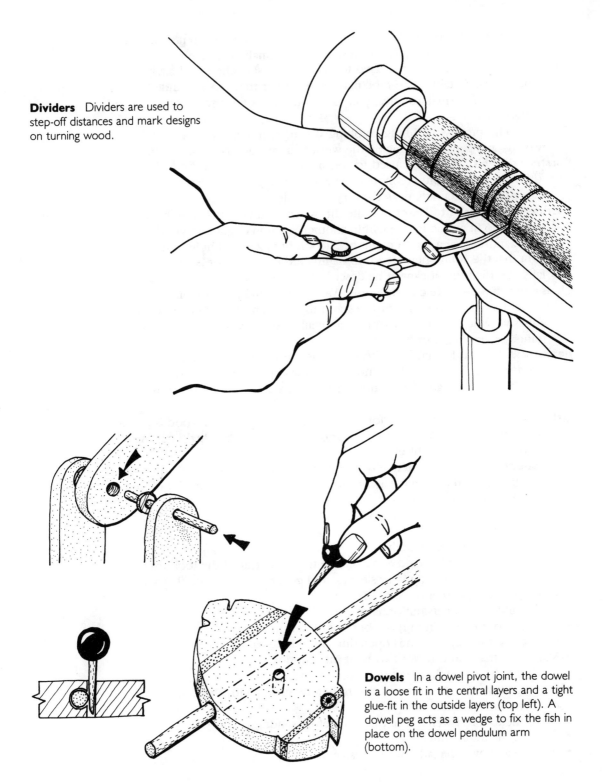

Dividers Dividers are used to step-off distances and mark designs on turning wood.

Dowels In a dowel pivot joint, the dowel is a loose fit in the central layers and a tight glue-fit in the outside layers (top left). A dowel peg acts as a wedge to fix the fish in place on the dowel pendulum arm (bottom).

large two-handed rasps. We tend to use open-toothed surform rasps for large jobs and sandpaper wrapped around sticks for small details.

filler   A soft putty-like material used to patch tears, scratches, and cavities. We prefer to use a stable, two-tube plastic-resin filler that can be sanded, sawn, and drilled. For small cavities, you can make a filler with scroll saw dust and PVA adhesive.

finishing   The process of filling, rubbing down, staining, painting, varnishing, waxing, and generally bringing the work to a satisfactory conclusion.

Forstner drill bit   A drill bit used for boring out flat-bottomed holes in wood. Although Forstner bits are more expensive than regular spade or flat drill bits, they produce accurate, perfect-every-time holes.

friction-fit or push-fit   Describes the fit when components can be pushed together to fit perfectly one within another. A tenon might be a good friction-fit in a mortise, or a dowel might be friction-fit in a wheel-hole. If the fit is so tight that the component needs to hammered into place or is so loose that it falls out, then the fit cannot be described as a push-fit.

glues and adhesives   We currently use PVA, or polyvinyl acetate, for large joints, dowel fixings, mating flat surfaces and the like, and Super Glue fast-drying adhesive when we need to make a small, fast, very strong, dab-and-hold joints. See **resin glue**.

headstock   In woodturning, the headstock is the power-driven unit at the left-hand side of the lathe. The central headstock spindle has an external screw thread for chucks and face plates, and an internal taper for the pronged center.

lathe   A woodworking machine for cutting round sections. The wood is pivoted between centers or held in a chuck and spun against a handheld cutting tool such as a gouge or a chisel.

lathe safety   The lathe is potentially an extremely dangerous piece of equipment. You always need to be wide awake and ready for the unexpected. Before you switch on the lathe, always:

- Wear safety glasses and a dust mask.
- Chose nontoxic wood.
- Mount the workpiece securely.
- Turn the work over by hand to make sure that it is clear of the tool rest.
- Tie back your hair, roll up your sleeves, and generally make sure that you aren't going to get dragged into the lathe.
- Keep children and pets out of harm's way.
- Place all your tools within reach but out of harm's way.
- Check that the stop switch is operating and within easy reach.
- Make sure that you can work without interruption.
  Once you have switched on the power, always:
- Stop the motor, or at least slow down, before testing with a template, dividers, or calipers.
- Move the tool rest well out of the way before sanding.
- Hold all the tools firmly.
- Never reach over the lathe while it is running.

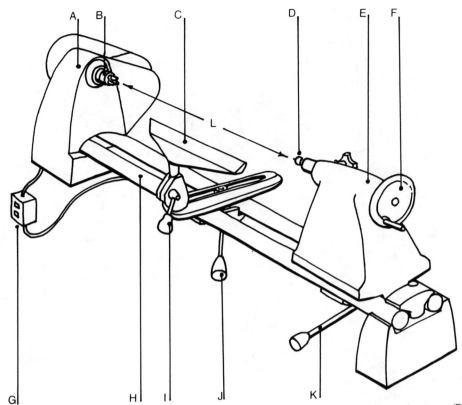

Lathe   (A) headstock, (B) spindle or drive center, (C) tool rest or T-rest, (D) tailstock center, (E) tailstock, (F) spindle-advance wheel, (G) power switch, (H) bed, (I) quick-release clamp for the rest, (J) quick-release clamp for the rest on the bed, (K) quick-release clamp for the tailstock, (L) distance between centers.

mating faces   The area between two touching parts, or two faces that are to be glued together, are described as mating faces.

maquette   see **prototype**

multicore plywood   For making toys, we always use best-quality, birch or white-faced, multicore or multiveneer plywood. Such a plywood is commonly sold in thicknesses ranging from 1/8 inch to 1 inch. Purchasing a whole 48-×-96-inch sheet, rather than small pieces, is more economical. If you can only afford a single sheet, buy the 1/4-inch-thick plywood and sandwich layers to make 1/2 inch, 3/4 inch, or whatever. Best-quality multicore plywood can be cut easily on a scroll saw, with all faces and edges worked to a smooth and even finish. Be warned—If you settle for cheap-grade, coarse-center plywood, it will be very difficult to work, and the laminations will probably break down and the cut edges will need filling.

offcuts   Bits and pieces of scrap wood left over from other projects that can be saved and used for small jobs and for making prototypes. Many wood suppliers sell very useful offcuts.

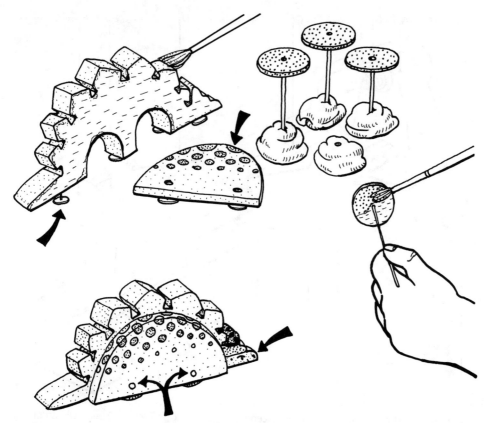

Painting Paint the ground, or base, color first, covering the edges and then the sides (top left). Hold the wheels on a dowel peg and support them on blobs of Plasticine (right and top right). Give the background color a light sanding and then paint the secondary details (middle). After assembly, touch up damaged areas with paint and then lay on the varnish (bottom).

painting Ideally, you should paint in an area that has been set apart for that purpose. We use acrylics, rather than model-maker's enamel or oil paints, because they are user-friendly and nontoxic. Acrylics dry very quickly, several coats of paint can be applied in a short time, the brushes can be washed in water, and the colors are bright. The order of work is:
1. Start by making sure that the object to be painted is smooth, clean, dry, and free from dust.
2. Spend time carefully setting out all your paints and materials.
3. Consider how the objects are going to be supported when they have been painted, and set up a line, wire rack, or whatever.
4. Lay on a couple of base or ground coats of matte acrylic paint.
5. Decorate with the fine-point details.
6. Finally, varnish, let dry, and wax.

painting grid color code Each of the painting grids has been coded with the colors of our choice.

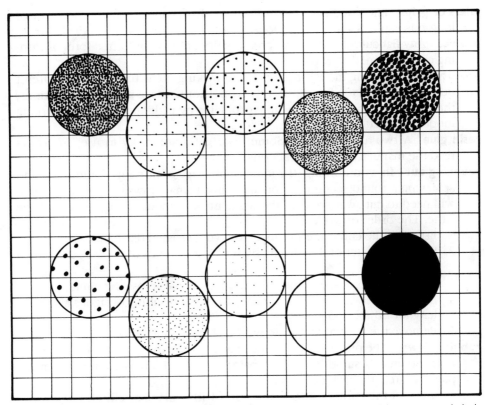

Painting grid color code Top row, left to right: red, light blue, blue, light green, and dark green. Bottom row, left to right: medium green, orange/gold, yellow, white, and black.

pencils and pencil-press transferring We use a soft 2B for designing and tracing and a hard H pencil for pencil-press transferring. The order of work is:
1. Draw out the full-sized master design.
2. Take a careful tracing.
3. Pencil in the lines at the back of the tracing with a 2B pencil.
4. Turn the tracing right side up and fix it to working surface of the wood with tabs of masking tape.
5. Finally, rework the traced lines with a hard pencil. The marks will transfer to the wood surface.

pillar drill or drill press A large, bench-mounted electric drill with a bit-gripping chuck and an adjustable-height and -angle worktable. If you plan on making a lot of toys, then such a drill is a very useful piece of machinery.

pilot hole A small, drilled guide hole through which the blade of the scroll saw can be passed, or a hole used to ensure an easy passage for a screw.

pivot A pivot is the point, rod, bolt, rivet, shaft, or dowel on which another part might swing, turn, roll, or otherwise move.

plane A hand-held tool used for smoothing and leveling wood. We use a small metal bench plane.

pliers or grips Pliers and grips come in many shapes and sizes. We use a pair of long-nosed pliers and a pair of locking grips.

profiles Any flat cutout, silhouette, cross section, drawn, or fretted form or turning can be termed a profile.

prototype A working model made prior to making the actual toy. If you aren't quite sure how a toy functions, or if you want to make a few modifications, then you need to iron out possible problems by making a mockup, working model, maquette, or prototype.

resin glue A two-tube adhesive. Some resin glues are tricky to use, so always read the manufacturer's instructions.

roughing out In woodturning, the initial swift stage of turning off the waste and achieving a round section. If you are using a small, low-powered lathe, you will need to cut away some of the waste prior to mounting the wood on the lathe. The order of work is:

1. Establish the end centerpoints by drawing crossed diagonals.
2. Set the diameter of the turning by scribing the ends of the wood out with circles.
3. Draw tangents at the points where the diagonals cross the circle.
4. Establish the waste by drawing lines from the resulting octagons along the length of the wood.
5. Remove the bulk of the waste with a plane or drawknife.

rubbing down The process of using sandpaper to rub the sawn profiles and sections down to a smooth, ready-to-paint finish. Working well away from the painting area, the order of work is:

1. Trim off the corners, edges, and burrs with a plane or chisel.
2. Swiftly rub over the piece with a medium-grit sandpaper.
3. Fill cracks or holes with two-tube resin filler.
4. Finally, work through the pack of coarse- to smooth-graded sandpapers until the workpiece is smooth to the touch.

Warning: If you are worried about breathing in potentially harmful dust, wear a mask.

sanding and sandpaper Purchase sandpapers in graded packs, with the grades running in degrees of coarseness, or grit, from rough to smooth. Small, difficult-to-reach areas are best worked with the sandpaper wrapped around a stick tool.

screws and screwdrivers In toymaking, screws are safer and more permanent than nails. If you have a choice, use brass screws with round or countersunk heads. When you are finishing, always make sure that the screws are smooth to the touch and free from sharp edges and burrs. Use the correct size screwdrivers to avoid doing damage to the workpiece and the screw.

scroll saw A fine-bladed, electric bench saw, sometimes called a jigsaw or fretsaw, used for cutting out profiles in thin sheet wood, plastic, or metal. Push the workpiece across the worktable and feed it into the blade. Blades come in many grades, and are cheap and easy to replace. The scroll saw is safe to use, as long as you hold the workpiece firmly down on the table, work at a steady pace, and always present the blade with the line of next cut. The up-and-

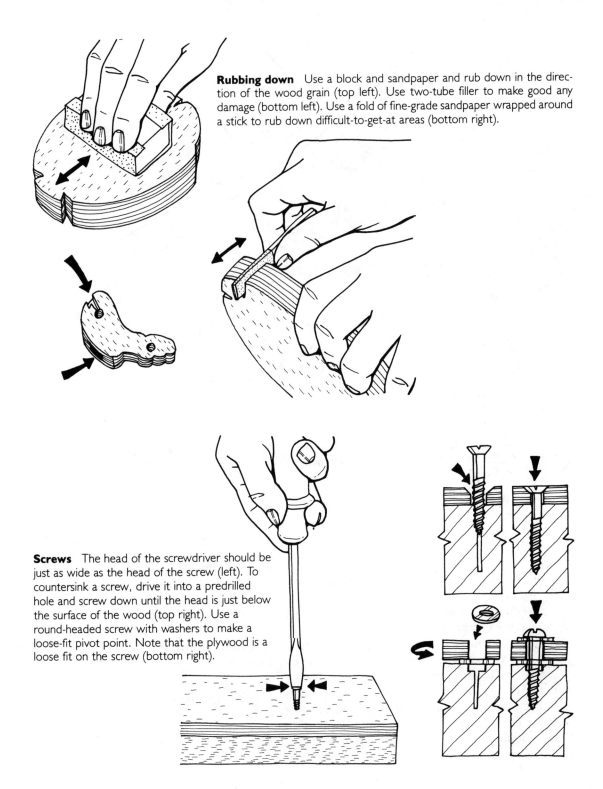

Rubbing down Use a block and sandpaper and rub down in the direction of the wood grain (top left). Use two-tube filler to make good any damage (bottom left). Use a fold of fine-grade sandpaper wrapped around a stick to rub down difficult-to-get-at areas (bottom right).

Screws The head of the screwdriver should be just as wide as the head of the screw (left). To countersink a screw, drive it into a predrilled hole and screw down until the head is just below the surface of the wood (top right). Use a round-headed screw with washers to make a loose-fit pivot point. Note that the plywood is a loose fit on the screw (bottom right).

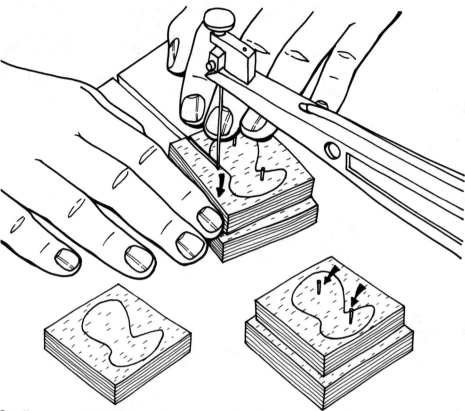

Scroll saw—multiple cutting Pencil-press transfer the traced design through to one thickness of the plywood, sandwich the layers together with pins, and cut through the whole sandwich.

down jigging action of the blade results in a swift, fine cut. Our scroll saw can cut anything from thin veneers through 2-inch-thick wood. It is the perfect tool for toymaking. The order of work for cutting out an enclosed hole or window is:

1. Release the blade tension and unhitch the top end of the blade.
2. Slide the workpiece on the cutting table and pass the blade through the pilot hole.
3. Refit the blade, adjust the tension, and make sure that the worktable is set at the correct angle.
4. Switch on the power and feed the wood into the blade so that the line of cut is slightly to the waste side of the drawn line.
5. Remove the waste and unhitch the blade.

Multiple cutting with the scroll saw is the process of stacking layers of plywood together and cutting out a number of identical profiles. For example, if the project calls for two identical legs, you sandwich two sheets of plywood together with pins or double-sided tape, cut through both layers at the same time, and then ease the layers apart and remove the temporary fixings.

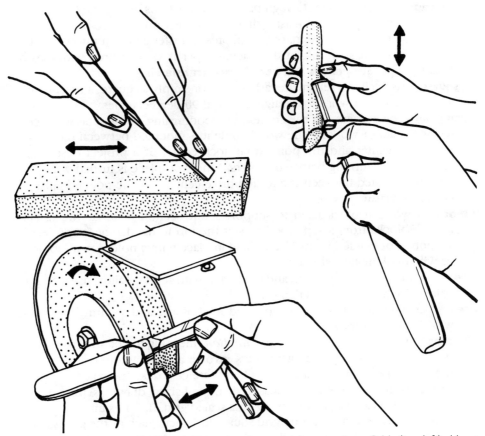

Sharpening tools Use an oilstone to bring the tool edge to a keen finish (top left). Use a shaped slipstone to hone the inside curve of a gouge (right). Use the grindstone to reshape a blunt or damaged edge (bottom left).

setting out Transferring the working drawings through to the face of the wood and making initial cuts. See **pencils and pencil-press transferring**.

sharpening tools All your cutting and edging tools need to be sharp. Ideally, you need a grindstone to reshape the bevel on a chipped or blunt edge, an oilstone for honing and rubbing down to a keen fine edge, and shaped slipstones to hone concave U-section gouges.

stick tools Any found item that might be used for supporting sandpaper is a stick tool. We tend to use such things as lollipop or popsicle sticks, broken hacksaw blades, and bits of dowel. Fix the sandpaper in place with pins or tape, and then hold and use like a file. See **sanding and sandpapers**.

straight saws Any straight, flat-bladed woodworking saw that does the job at hand.

template A pattern or shape cut from thin-sheet wood or cardboard that can be drawn around to reproduce a number of identical images.

tracing paper   A strong, see-through paper used for transferring the lines of the design from the full-sized master drawing to the working face of the wood. When you trace off a design, or pencil-press transfer a design through to the wood, always make sure that the tracing paper is well secured with tabs of masking tape. See **pencils and pencil-press transferring**.

try square   Also called a set square, a T square, or simply a square, a try square is a tool used to test work for straightness and 90-degree angles.

turning between centers   In the context of woodturning, turning between centers is the act of working the wood while it is mounted between the forked headstock center and the pointed tailstock center. If a project describes a technique as ''turning between centers,'' the workpiece is turned while it is held and pivoted between the forked drive center and the pointed tailstock center. See **lathe**.

V-block   A wooden block used to support round-section material. We usually make V-blocks from scrap wood to suit the job in hand. The workpiece is supported or cradled in the V, and held in place with a hold-down foot loop or with masking-tape strapping.

varnish   For toys that are painted and decorated with acrylic paints, use a clear or golden, high-gloss polyurethane varnish.

vise   A bench-mounted screw clamp, used for holding and securing the wood while it is being worked.

whittling   From the Anglo-Saxon word *thwitan*, meaning to cut and pare with a small knife. Many toymaking projects involve a small amount of whittling: slices are taken from turnings, dowel ends are cut back, and so on.

working drawings   The scaled, measured, or full-sized drawings from which measurements are taken; a drawing on a scaled grid. If, for example, the scale of the grid is described as one grid square to 1 inch, each of the grid squares can be transferred as 1 square inch. If you want to change the scale, all you do is draw up a different grid and transfer the image one square at a time.

working face   In the context of this book, the working face is the best side of the wood, the side that shows once the toy has been put together.

workout paper   Paper on which all the project notes, details, and sketches are done prior to actually working with the wood. We use a hardcover sketch book for all the initial designs and small details, and lengths of end-of-roll printer's paper or decorator's paper for the full-sized patterns. Try to save all your patterns for the next time around.

Index